LIFE LESSONS FROM A 40 SOMETHING...

By Pamela Sommers

Money

The information contained within this book is strictly for educational purposes. If you wish to apply ideas contained in this book, you are taking full responsibility for your actions.

The author has made every effort to ensure the accuracy of the information within this book was correct at the time of publication. The author does not assume and hereby disclaims any liability to any party for any loss, damage, or disruption caused by errors or omissions, whether such errors or omissions result from accident, negligence, or any other cause.

This represents general information only. Before making any financial or investment decisions, I recommend you consult a financial planner to take into account your personal investment objectives, financial situation, and individual needs.

General

This book is designed to provide information and motivation to the reader. It is sold with the understanding that the author is not engaged to render any type of psychological, legal, or any other kind of professional advice. The content of each article is the sole expression and opinion of its author. No warranties or guarantees are expressed or implied by the author's choice to include any of the content in this volume. The individual author shall not be liable for any physical, psychological, emotional, financial, or commercial damages, including, but not limited to, special, incidental, consequential or other damages. Please be advised that you are responsible for your own choices, actions, and results.

I dedicate this book to my son,

Reece Sommers.

I hope it helps you through your journey in life and inspires you to follow your dreams.

'The world is your oyster.'

I love you always.

CONTENTS

PREFACE

Over the years there have been many times where I wished I had someone (other than my parents) to ask for guidance and who would share their words of wisdom with me. By the same token, I must confess, because I am self-sufficient and headstrong, I may not necessarily have taken the advice, let alone listened to it. However, now that I am in my forties, I can see things with much more calmness and clarity, and upon reflection, I wish I had paid more attention.

Throughout my life, I have experienced different roles: a troubled and somewhat rebellious teenager, a daughter, a sister, a friend, a girlfriend, a wife, and a mother. Each of these roles has led me to have experiences that I never thought I would have, but in turn, I have learnt many lessons from. Some I have to admit were hard and painful, while others were filled with extreme happiness.

There have been times where I have said to myself, 'I wish I knew this earlier' or 'I wish I had been able to ask my mother' (but, alas, she is no longer with us).

Perhaps I would have done things differently or made different decisions. Perhaps I would have walked a little taller, had a little more confidence, spoken a little louder, and believed in myself a little more.

This book is for you if you want to get the best out of life from early on. It is a note to my younger self about the things I wish I had known earlier on in my life. I hope that it helps you along your journey of life by saving you time and preventing pain and heartache; I don't want you to go through things the hard way. This book helps you through everyday matters. It discusses the things most people don't talk about, such as you staying positive while the environment around you seems negative. It will also offer practical advice on how to manage your money; I am sharing with you the best practices I have learnt from my financial experiences, including my time as a manager in retail banking, my working life, and as a current business owner of an award-winning company. But, of course, before you focus on building your wealth, it is essential to maintain your health too, as this is what will keep you going. I have included topics about this, because, in my experience, the mind, body, and spirit are all magnificently connected.

Life is a voyage of self-discovery, and there will always be new things to learn as we take in all the experiences life has to offer. It is a gift that should be treasured, appreciated, and celebrated. At times it may not be easy; there will be lows as well as highs, but you are not alone.

I hope this book will feel as though someone is holding your hand through it all. Let's take the first step together by putting one foot in front of the other; let's enjoy the journey...

CHAPTER 1

JUST BE YOU

When you are young, you think you will be young forever and growing old is way off in the distance. You are bursting with energy, dreams, and imagination. You are willing to take risks and leap into action within a moment. You don't need to feel prepared and are more than willing to jump in with both feet first.

Then, as you become older, you start to realise that life isn't as smooth sailing as that. It can take you by surprise, and it can even leave you feeling bewildered at times. But this doesn't have to be the case if you are prepared for the unexpected. With a little guidance, positive intention, and willingness, you can be all that you want to be and more.

We all require role models to look up to for inspiration and guidance. This being said, you may not want to talk to or even approach your parents, carers, or other family members, and I don't blame you. I recall that when I was a teenager, my parents would be the last people I turned to. Most of the time because I was afraid of them (hitting children was allowed in those days, and as the eldest child, I got more than my fair share, I can tell you). However, respecting your parents was a 'big' deal back then, and nowadays parents try different techniques; some even try to be your 'friend'.

Some people (i.e. your parents) may call you "selfish" because you appear to dive into things without giving thought to consequences and the effects it may have on others. This may be true, but what do they know? They simply don't understand (at least that's what I thought). After all, you've probably heard it time and time again when people say, "the world doesn't revolve around you, you know". But quite frankly, from a young person's point of view, if not you, then who? You only have one life, and you want to make it the best it can be. As you can only see life from one perspective, well, then of course life revolves around you. I mean, who else can think the way you do? Who else has your humour or tells your story the way you can?

That's right; there's no one else who can be you. We are all unique, and we all have good points about us and inevitably not-so-good points.

Nobody's perfect, and we should never aspire to

be perfect. That is pressure in itself. Yes, there is so much pressure on young people growing up. There is pressure to conform to the majority, peer pressure, media pressure, and we now have the added pressure of social media. But as soon as we accept that there is no such thing as perfection, the less pressure we will feel. Once we relax, we will find that we can just be…

Sometimes people are afraid to just 'be', so they just 'do' all the time.

For instance, try turning off your phone at night and see how you feel. This is unheard of for most people. They don't want to miss out. What are they missing out on really? Is it really worth having disturbed sleep? We all require an adequate amount of rest for our mind and bodies to recharge and regenerate. To 'be' at our best, we need to 'feel' our best. Begin by giving yourself a head start each day and allow yourself to rest and just be.

CHAPTER 2

ENOUGH

You are enough

A newborn baby is perfect and pure in every way, no matter what weight or colour it is. It has no flaws and is free from influences and all bad things. You were once a newborn baby – free from negativity and criticism.

Our surroundings and influencers help mould us into what we become and into what we believe. When we are young, we are naturally influenced by our parents or carers or those close to us. They are usually the first people we come into contact with, and they are usually the first people we trust and assume have our best interests at heart. Most of the time this is true, but sadly, in some cases, this doesn't happen.

Most parents do the best they can. They encourage their children, praise them, and help them to stay focused and motivated. They also pat them on the back, show them appreciation, and love them unconditionally, regardless of if they fail or succeed. Most parents say positive things about their children, and, without a doubt, these children know that they are supported by their parents and that their parents have their back 100%.

But what about the ones who don't? The ones who aren't encouraged or supported by their parents? The ones who are unsure whether they can rely on their parents? What if the parents praise their siblings and not them? Or even worse, what if the parent puts the person down, constantly criticises him or her, and calls them, 'stupid' many times, or even worse, calls him or her names and swears at them constantly?

What kind of message do you think that is telling a child?

I was that child.

If you were or are that child, let me make it clear to you right now: you are enough.

I remember comparing myself to my best friend, who had parents who always encouraged her, and asking my mum when I was 14: "Mum, how come Lesley's parents always encourage her and you never do?" My mother turned, looked at me, and said, "That's because I want you to try harder."

Yes, it answered my question, but then it dawned on me that my parents thought that by not encouraging me and putting me down that they were, in fact, helping me, but it didn't help me to feel more confident. I didn't feel like I could do anything I dreamed of.

To be honest, my parents probably never realised the effect it had on me, just like you probably don't know what your parents were going through during the time you were growing up. They were probably going through their own personal struggles and wrestling with their own issues. Unfortunately, there are no guides to good parenting really. What works for one family may not work for another.

You can't change the past; forgiveness, regardless of whether you understand it or not, will help you remove this feeling of unworthiness. It will release you from the chains of criticism and will help you live your life feeling lighter and loved. It probably will take time, but you have to forgive to be able to move forward in your own life. If your parents are no longer around now, forgive them mentally and notice the change in yourself.

It took me many years to understand and believe this, but it really makes a difference when you can get these feelings under control and let it work for you in a positive way.

Yes, your parents didn't know any better and probably would behave differently now or maybe they wouldn't. It doesn't matter. If anything, it has taught me not to look for reassurance from others. Trust your inner guidance.

It's okay to be yourself

While you are growing up, you may feel the need to try and become more popular with those around you. Many people try and fit into what they think is the norm. As children, there is pressure to be like everyone else. This happens at school, too. Teachers and people of authority want everyone to follow the norm to make it easier for them, and a lot of the time they do not want this questioned. Yes, life probably would be a lot easier if everyone were the same, especially if they thought the same, spoke in a similar way, dressed in a similar style, and didn't do anything to upset the system.

But everyone is not the same. We are all unique. Each person has his or her own thoughts and opinions, speaks in his or her own voice, and dresses in his or her own way. Life would probably be boring if we were all the same.

Some people are afraid of being themselves; they worry that they won't be liked or they won't fit into a group or belong to a club. In fact, they spend so much time worrying about what other people think that they overlook their own qualities.

You are unique, and yes, you are different, and you don't need permission from others to be yourself. Stop seeking it.

Embrace your flaws and your weaknesses, as long as you also remember to embrace your qualities, your talents, and your strengths. These all help to make up who you are.

You are beautiful – remember that

When I was a child, I remember my mother calling me an 'Ugly Duckling'. I can't recall if I overheard her saying it to someone or if she said it directly to me. On another occasion, I showed her a school photo of all the class and asked her who she thought was the prettiest. She pointed at me in the photo. I said, "But I can't be." She confirmed that she thought I was. Guess which memory I remember the most? If I really thought I was beautiful growing up – let me re-phrase that, if I really BELIEVED I was beautiful growing up – I am sure I would have been more confident, walked taller, and spoke out more.

I was speaking to a mature lady one day, and we were looking through photos of her when she was younger. I said she looked beautiful. She said to me, "Do you know I didn't realise I was beautiful until I was much older after someone mentioned it. I wish they had told me sooner." Unfortunately, she is no longer with us, but what a sad thought: to go through life not realising you are beautiful.

CHAPTER 3

YOU ARE NOT ALONE

Loneliness

There may be times in your life when you feel alone, I mean utterly alone. The kind of loneliness where you could be in a crowded room and still feel as if you are on your own. Does that sound familiar to you?

I have had this feeling many times, especially as a young adult. It didn't matter whom I was with, it felt a little like a bottomless hole that I couldn't see out of. The good thing about darkness though is that there is always the possibility of light showing up. At times, you need to look for these flashes of light. They may appear when you least expect it, and when you do find them, hold on to them and don't let them go. Enjoy the experience, and don't be afraid to smile. For this brings more light into the darkness, which in turn brings more light around you and into this world. Know that you are not alone. Many, many people feel loneliness. You may find some people do not want to admit this, but that could be because they are fighting their own personal battles. It may be that they are too afraid to face their fears because it reminds them of their weaknesses or something they are trying to escape from. Don't worry about them; everyone has to do things at a time that is right for them. We all have our own personal journey to explore. What is right for you may not be right for another because we are all unique and have different abilities, interests, and opinions.

For instance, I know someone who absolutely hates being by herself. If she finds no one is at home when she gets in, she immediately turns around and walks back out. She panics if she is left alone, possibly due to a fear of feeling lonely. She worries she is missing out on things, hates working alone in an office, feels the need to be surrounded by people constantly, and enjoys lots of noise, whereas I would find that quite draining. I can be very sociable for short periods, and then I gradually start to crave my own space and like to go off somewhere quiet where I feel I can 'breathe' now and again.

Yes, there will be good times, and there will also be times when you feel low. This will pass because everything is temporary. You will feel like you belong and that you are enough, and you will feel happy again.

CHAPTER 4

COMPARING

Don't compare yourself to others

I am sure we are all guilty of this at some point in our lives. As children, we want what the other child has, especially if it's bigger, brighter, shinier, and the latest toy or game. We pester and put pressure on our parents to get that toy for us because someone in the same class has it. We want to go to a party because the other kids in our class are going.

Adults are just as guilty of this. For instance, if a neighbour has had a home renovation done, we want to get something done to our house. Even in business, someone can't understand how that new business is getting all the customers while he or she has been around for years and are not getting that footfall. This occurs when people get jealous and want a piece of the action. It can be very frustrating and will keep you going around in circles - if you let it.

The thing is if you are focusing on what others have instead of what you have, it leads you into a vicious circle where you start being negative not just to others but also to yourself.

Everyone has their own abilities, qualities, and times of success and good fortune. There is plenty to go around. It may well be the right time for them, but that doesn't mean your time won't come. You too will have you time to shine.

Try enjoying the good things, and even though it may sound crazy, get to know yourself more. Imagine you are meeting yourself for the first time. Spend time by yourself, discovering what you like and what you don't like. Ask yourself questions in your mind. For instance, what makes you laugh? What do you enjoy doing? What do you dislike doing? This is all part of loving yourself for the person you are and trusting yourself as well as believing in yourself. For when you believe in yourself, you have no reason to question your abilities or doubt yourself by thinking others are better than you.

A useful exercise is to make a list of all the great qualities you have and include what you are good at, too. This may seem hard at first because we are seldom used to saying good things about ourselves, but once you practice this several times, soon you will have the hang of it. It may take you a few days to do this, and as you keep adding to the list, you will probably find out things about yourself that you forgot you could do. After writing this down, be sure to read it through to yourself regularly; not only will this act as a reminder of all the accomplishments you have achieved, but you will also start believing the good things about yourself, which will hopefully make you feel a lot better about yourself. Try it and see.

Before long, you will find that you do not need to keep looking to others for approval or guidance on what to do next because you will start trusting in your own abilities and you won't feel the need to compare yourself to others.

CHAPTER 5

TRUST YOUR JUDGEMENT

Trust your instincts

Listen to your intuition and trust what you are feeling. This can take practice as well as patience; be in touch with your feelings so much that you notice even the slightest negative feeling towards a person, idea, or thought.

There have been occasions in my life where I have gone against what I was feeling at the time and wish I hadn't. Take the time, for example, when I went for an interview for a job, and for some reason, I couldn't put my finger on it, but I didn't take to the person who I would be working with. I felt she was rather arrogant and seemed a bit like a gang leader and used to her own little crowd around her. Don't get me wrong; she was extremely friendly and lovely to my face, and we got on really well once I started working with her. It wasn't until months later that I started seeing her other side come out. She talked about me unfavourably to others. I heard this myself, and when I confronted her, she, of course, denied it and said I was too oversensitive. There were other occasions where she tried to blame me for things. It was quite sad really because I had genuinely thought we had a lovely friendship, but, alas, I was mistaken and realised that I should have trusted my initial feelings about her. But, hey-ho, you live and learn.

I now know without hesitation that if you trust your intuition, it can save a lot of pain and heart-ache in the long run. Time is too precious for regrets, so save time and pain and just go with your feelings about a situation.

Trust your judgement

You know the difference between wrong and right. You know when you are being led astray, and as you make that decision about an activity or someone, remember that you know yourself better than anyone else does. Do what feels right; just make sure you will still feel good about it afterwards. If there's a good chance you would regret it, well, then I think you know which choice to make. Go with your gut feeling.

Don't trust everyone you meet

It is sad to say, but it's best you find out now and not at the expense of your time, your heart, and also your pride. Not everyone who befriends you will be genuine. Some will be out for what they can get. Some will use you to benefit themselves in some way. They may use you as a stepping-stone along a career path or because you have connections. They could also try and use you in a romantic way if they have something to gain from it. This may sound harsh, but, as I have found through my working life, it is true. They may be really nice to your face, but the moment they think you aren't around, they will say unpleasant things about you to make them look good.

This doesn't have to be a colleague; it could also be from someone in management. Once he or she realises you have discovered his or her true colours, you probably won't hear much from them. I have, unfortunately, found this out in all different types of job roles and from different people who I thought were 'my friends', like the example of the interview I went to. This reiterates that you should trust your first instincts about people and learn to trust your judgement and to rely on yourself. Yes, it can be a lonely feeling, and it isn't a pleasant one, but it will help to have your wits about you in the long run.

Don't be naïve in thinking everyone has your best interests in mind. Trust your instincts; you have them for a reason. Have your wits about you. Be nice and polite, but as soon as you think someone is trying to take advantage of you, let them know that you are aware of what they are doing in the nicest way possible. There's no need to be nasty; keep calm and remain dignified. Do things with a little panache, style, finesse, and class. Don't allow yourself to sink down to the other person's level because chances are that is what they want. They want to provoke you so that you look like the bad person.

This reminds me of when I was about eight years old. There was a girl looked similar to a 'Sindy' doll. She was so pretty, but she wasn't very nice to me. She used to keep antagonising me until one time when I thought enough was enough. She wouldn't let me pass and blocked the doorway of a classroom. She kept saying "no" and kept goading me. In the end, I did something that was completely out of character for me. I punched her in the stomach and passed through the doorway. While others gathered around her, I ran and sat crying on a bench far away in the playground. I felt awful. Even though she had been provoking me for months, I felt like a really bad person. Then a friend came over to see why I was crying. I told her, and she said that the other girl was absolutely fine. Funnily enough, she even came up to me and deeply apologised for her behaviour over the past months and started giggling. She seemed to 'respect' me and asked if we could be friends. Ironically, we became really good friends afterwards.

I'm not suggesting that you punch everyone who provokes or taunts you; I was a child back then and realise that violence is never justified unless it's in self-defence. What I am saying is that, as an adult, there are ways to let people know in a short, sharp sentence that you are not putting up with the behaviour (without resorting to violence). It could even be said with a little humour with a smile on your face, so the other person doesn't realise it immediately, but then the penny drops. Then they back off because they realise they can't mess with you. You know this now so you are equipped.

There are jealous people out there

When I was at school, there used to be a girl called Anna. She was known for being jealous; she always wanted her own way, and she just seemed to be full of herself. She was very smug, and she used to get top marks regularly. I also got high marks so that didn't really bother me. But I could never understand why she was often nasty to me. She even called me "stupid" once. I quickly retorted that I wasn't stupid, and I think she was surprised by that. Just because I was quiet, it didn't mean that I was going to put up with remarks like that, especially as I used to hear them from my father as a child (probably out of habit). I soon realised that she probably felt threatened by me.

I saw many other examples of people who were jealous while I grew up, but she was one of the first people that I found to be jealous at an early age.

Jealousy can come in all different forms, but it doesn't always have to be bad. For instance, if you find yourself being jealous of someone, question what you are jealous of and why. Jealousy is a primal instinct and can actually work for you by bringing to the surface what you really want or what is important to you. The important thing is to try to control and manage your jealousy so it doesn't take over your life or spill into other areas (i.e. your relationships). It helps just to know that jealous people do exist, and sometimes there will be people who are jealous of you or the lifestyle you have. Don't be surprised if these people are close to you.

There are also good-natured people out there

On the flip-side, there are some lovely people out there who just want to bring good wherever they go. They are beacons of light and are a blessing to have around. They don't ask for anything in return except your company. Look after these people for they are like a rare flower. Treat them with the respect they deserve and listen to what they have to say. Show them you appreciate them: perhaps treat them to dinner, coffee, or even a trip to a health spa. Show them your love and how much they mean to you. Many of these people have learnt and endured many lessons along the way and are very wise. I wonder if you can think of someone like that right now? And I bet it brings a smile to your face.

Racism is real and may also be from those you least expect

My parents were from Mauritius and came over in the late 60s to train as nurses. They actually met while they were in training. Rather romantic, I think. In those days, more people showed their prejudices.

My parents were pretty modern compared to other traditional immigrants of Asian descent.

I was very confident and outgoing as a toddler and spent a lot of time in Mauritius, even though I was born in Greenwich, England. In the UK, when I was 6 years old, I went to a Church of England infants' school. I was a very quiet child in the UK compared to how I behaved in Mauritius. My dad taught me to be quiet and get on with it. I wasn't shy; I was just quiet.

I remember two girls asked me to play; they had long, blonde hair and blue eyes. Their names were Tina and Samantha. I was so happy to be asked to play that I said "yes."

They took me into the toilets and washed my arms with toilet water (after it was flushed); they said they were trying to wash the dirt off and make me clean.

That was the first time I noticed my colour!

Nothing like that ever happened again as a child. While I was growing up, I discovered I wasn't like other brown-skinned teenagers. My parents were modern, and I loved them for it. My mother had short hair and wore skirts and dresses. She was outspoken and loved to laugh. My parents loved having parties and were very sociable – the life and soul of the party. Is it any wonder we (my sisters and I) grew up to be so independent and determined?

I have found that racism can come in different forms and from anyone, including people of a similar ethnic background.

I used to get told, "she thinks she's white" and

even received verbal abuse once from a lady after she spoke to me in a different language. When I didn't understand her, she accused me of lying. To top it all off, I dyed my hair a lot and even got blonde high-lights, which possibly didn't help matters.

To be honest, I forget my colour in everyday life. I am just me, but I'm not so naïve to think that racism doesn't exist.

Learn the power of 'no'

Many people go through life being afraid of saying no. They worry about what people will think of them; they worry they won't have any friends and that nobody will like them. Normally these people are people-pleasers. They put others first with total disregard for themselves. The thing is, this soon takes a toll on their spirit, their health, and their life. They could even start feeling resentful, and, despite this, they still continue to say yes. This may be an employee trying to please his or her boss; or someone saying they are 'helping' their family or friends, but the truth of the matter is that they are afraid of what may happen if they say 'no'. I think some of these people live in fear. They lack self-respect for themselves, because, by constantly pleasing others before themselves, they are not valuing themselves as a person.

Have some self-respect. What's the worst that could happen? People will probably think you have finally got some courage and stood up for yourself. Be assertive now and then; some people may not like it, but at least you value yourself enough to realise that your time is also precious. You are precious. Stop acting the martyr and being resentful. If you are guilty of this, learn to say 'no' now and start creating boundaries. You may even start to feel good about yourself. You don't have to be nasty about it. Just don't be the type of person who says 'yes' all the time. Don't be a doormat and that goes for relationships as well. It's all very well being the 'nice' one, but some people take advantage of this.

This happened to me as a young adult, particularly with a boyfriend I had. I was basically infatuated with him; I wanted to please him and thought we would get married, but he basically used me and, looking back, I guess I allowed him to. I think my self-esteem was so low, that I was just happy to have a boyfriend, but, to be honest, he just wanted to keep me a secret. My mother tried to warn me several times, but I wouldn't listen and clung to him as much as I could. I suppose he did love me in his own way, but it wasn't a type of love that was good for my soul and spirit, not the way I needed to be loved. Truth be told, I probably spent more time crying than being happy. In later years, I bumped into him, and he apologised for how badly he treated me and said I deserved better. I did.

I have learnt this the hard way. As an adult, I sure didn't make the same mistake again. More often than not, I said 'no', especially if an employer was asking unreasonable things from me without any notice. I remember a female colleague once said to me, "I wish I was brave like you."

I replied, "what do you mean?"

She said, "I mean, you are so assertive; you just say 'no'. I wish I had the courage to do that."

I was quietly pleased because as a child I never stuck up for myself. I remember a school report I received when I was 10 or 11 that said: "She must learn to stand up for herself more." I guess I finally did.

Create boundaries

There is absolutely no need to stay in emotionally draining relationships, whether they are romantic or platonic. A sign of this is when you feel completely exhausted after you have been in touch with or near these people. Sometimes they don't even realise they have this effect on you. To protect and safeguard yourself from these people and situations, it is better to create boundaries rather than totally cut them off.

Make it clear what is okay for them to ask of you and what isn't. Sometimes things are unclear, and it is up to us to set these standards. No one else will do this for you. It can only be done by you.

For instance, you may have a friend who calls you constantly asking for advice at all times of the day and night. Set times for when he or she can call and switch your phone off at other times or don't answer the other calls. This will be hard at first, as it is a new habit and routine to get into. But once you get the hang of it, you will find it becomes easier. The other person may well start 'throwing their toys out the pram', so to speak, but they'll get over it. People don't like change, and that's all it is. Don't be the person at everyone's beck and call; it will wear you out, and you won't have the energy to put into your own projects and your own life. Your friend will probably respect you more in the long run too.

I mentioned romantic relationships. At first, it is natural to try and please your intended because you want to win him or her over and 'like' you, and part of that process is sacrificing what you like or your time to take on what they love. But be careful there; look for warning signs early on in the relationship. Look for signs of jealousy, mistrust, controlling behaviours, and if he or she wants to know exactly what you are doing every minute of the day. Some even get jealous if you give attention to other members of your family. Make it clear from the start and try to be honest about the type of person that you are; that way you both go into the relationship with eyes wide open.

Which is why you need to look out for these signs early on and avoid these situations. This is where you should learn to trust your judgement about people and follow your instincts. They will stand you in good stead throughout your life. You may be lucky enough to have loved ones to warn you, but what if you ignore their advice? So make it easy, and practice tuning into your instincts and judgement.

Only surround yourself with positive people— people who support and encourage your success. That way you know they have only the best intentions. 'Bad company corrupts good character' (1 Corinthians 15:33 NIV® Bible). So try and establish connections with positive people. You can tell when you are in their company as you will feel uplifted, happy, and will have plenty of energy.

Be respectful of yourself and your time, value yourself, and you will find others will do likewise.

CHAPTER 6

LOVE YOURSELF

Show yourself some love

This is probably one of the most valuable lessons you can learn, and it may sound obvious, but if you have a habit of putting others first, then you are not truly loving yourself.

How can you expect others to show you love when you don't even show love to yourself? How you treat yourself sets an example of how others see you and therefore treat you. It doesn't matter who they are, even if it is your parents or siblings, no one has a right to belittle you or make you feel uncomfortable about being yourself. Sometimes people call it 'banter', but is it really? They call it this because it covers a multitude of sins and gets them off the hook for their behaviour. If it doesn't make you feel good and you feel guilty for being yourself, either let them know diplomatically or, if it is in the workplace, speak to someone in authority. You deserve to be treated better. If you let it go, whether it's a member of your family or a colleague, it will happen again, so end it now.

If it helps, write down 10 things that you love about yourself and keep this list in a place you can access it whenever you need some reassurance or a boost. At first, you may find it hard to think of anything, but you'll soon get the hang of it. The next month, add 10 more things to the list. Soon you will be unstoppable and proud of yourself.

By the same token, list your achievements for the week or the month. I bet you've got a few already. This will help you realise that you have a lot going for you and you are worthy of being loved.

Take yourself out regularly, and do something you love, whether it's shopping, going to the gym or cinema, or even taking yourself out for a meal. Even think of going away by yourself now and again; you will be surprised by how much good this can do you. I did this a couple of times, and I was so energised, and it did wonders for my morale. I didn't feel alone at all and made lots of friends, which I probably wouldn't have met if I had company. Doing these things will help you feel good and help you realise the qualities you have as a person.

Go on, show yourself some love once in a while; you'll be so glad you did.

Respect yourself

It is so important to have some self-respect. After all, if you don't respect yourself, you can't expect others to.

How you treat yourself gives out clear signals to others about how they can treat you. Even though you can't see these signals, they have a habit of coming out.

For instance, it could be that you have a habit of always putting others before yourself, or maybe you are working for peanuts when you could be valuing yourself and your time more. I'm not saying to quit your job, but perhaps you should start looking for something that is more aligned to what you should be doing.

Maybe you are trying to impress a girlfriend or boyfriend and are always doing what they enjoy. If now and again you change it up and share something you enjoy, you could be happily surprised. It is better to show the real you now rather than later down the line. If he or she doesn't like it, you were obviously not meant to be.

Even though we may try to hide who we really

are at times—for instance, our likes and dislikes—life has a habit of letting your true colours out, whether you like it or not. It is far better to be real about who you are and what you do and don't like. People are drawn to the authenticity of others. It seems many haven't realised that because so many people put on an 'act' to please others. It is rare and also refreshing to finally find someone who is true to themselves. This goes for friends, colleagues, neighbours, and everyone you meet. Yes, you will find people who don't like you or share your opinions or beliefs, but they probably also respect you for being true to who you are.

How you value yourself, the style of clothes you wear, the food you choose to eat, and the lifestyle choices you make can say a lot about whether you show yourself respect. There have been many times, particularly in relationships where one person may play a 'victim' role and say they have been treated like 'a doormat'. Perhaps they have been perceived a certain way and have accepted it. Unfortunately, there are people out there that are only too happy to take advantage of someone or a situation to benefit themselves. This is a heart-breaking fact I'm afraid. Don't let that person be you. Look out for warning signs, such as being taken for granted, being lied to, and taken as a fool. You may even feel used. If this is the case, end the relationship as soon as you can. He or she won't change and even if they change later, don't allow yourself to be their target practice. You deserve so much better than that.

Show that you value yourself, and you will start to find that others do, too.

Be kind to yourself

It's so easy to be kind to others and forget about yourself. We are brought up to put others before ourselves by our parents and by schools. Many are taught 'think of others before yourself'. That's all very well and certainly helps society for the majority of the time, but what about the people who take advantage of this and are even unkind in return?

When you are nice to someone, it is a sad thought, but you may not always get the same treatment back. You have to be nice and kind to yourself and give yourself a break because you are doing the best you can.

Don't be too hard on yourself; there are many people who will be quick to judge you and criticise you. Do not help them by punishing yourself. The exercise where you list your qualities will also help you to see the good in you and to take it easy on yourself. I don't mean don't be disciplined; just don't beat yourself up over something you can't control.

Be gentle with yourself, and a little kindness towards yourself can go a long way. Try it and see. No one has a right to judge or be harsh with you, even though many will try. Don't let someone take that smile off your face. You deserve to be happy, and you deserve to smile.

Think happy thoughts, and do the things that bring you the most joy. Be that ray of sunshine in your life; wake up with a spring in your step. There is no harm in being optimistic about life, and you do not need permission from others to feel good about yourself or to feel good about your life.

Ask for help when you need it

There will be times where you simply can't do certain things or when it's beyond your expertise. For instance, if an appliance has broken down, and you need it fixed. At these times, you shouldn't be afraid to ask others for help; after all, we were not put on this earth alone. We have company, and so many people who are willing to help if we just let them.

It is not admitting defeat or giving in. It is being real and knowing your limits. When you are aware of this, you will realise just what you are capable of, and you will appreciate and value what others have to offer as well. Who knows? You may even help someone feel good about themselves. So, don't be afraid of calling out when you need a hand.

Be patient

Show yourself some love and be patient with yourself, with others, and with situations that arise. Everyone seems to be in a hurry and eager to rush things. The media adds to this with wanting you to have everything now. Many shops persuade people to 'buy now and pay later'. But you know life isn't really like that. Sometimes it's better to wait. I have known people who have taken their time, and, as a result, their lives have been saved. For instance, someone I know was taking it easy and was in no particular hurry to get to work one day. This was when the 7/7 catastrophe occurred in London when the bombs went off on the London bus and tube in the middle of the rush hour. Luckily for her, it was a good thing to be late, as who knows what could have occurred. I'm not suggesting you are deliberately late for work, but that sometimes things happen for a reason, and we just have to go with it. If you are in tune with your instincts and better judgement, this should be easier for you.

The older I become, the more I realise that

everything is temporary and nothing, including bad things, last forever, even though it may feel like it at the time. Bad times always pass.

So the next time you are eager for a situation or circumstance to end so that you can move on, just trust that it will, because you know what? It will.

Developing patience can take time, excuse the pun, but it's true. Some people are better at being patient than others. However, it can be learnt, and it will help you to be more aware of yourself and of others. It is a gift and will help you not only to look at a situation from a fresh perspective, but it will also help you to feel better about yourself. You don't have to go through life feeling stressed and rushing around like a headless chicken, flapping around in circles. Try a calmer approach, and see what happens.

Let it go

People tend to be weighed down and burdened a lot lately. They feel trapped and think that they have no choice or control over their lives or circumstances. They blame their job, their spouse, society, and everything and everyone around them.

But have you thought about how you are the common denominator in all of this? You see no one can control your thoughts or feelings. You are not a robot. You are human. Stop giving your power away to others. When you take control and take action, you often start to find that life has a new perspective. You start to see things differently. How you view things greatly influences how and what you choose to believe.

There is no use putting unnecessary pressure on yourself. Choose to see it in a different way. Unburden yourself and lighten your load. We cannot control everything; sometimes things just happen through no fault of your own. Let it go.

It isn't easy to take this approach; oftentimes we are so wrapped in our little worlds, we fail to see the effect our actions have on others around us. When you learn to let things go once in a while, this alleviates the pressure, albeit only for a little while.

When you feel lighter about life, you are more expansive and have more creative potential. When this happens, you allow new ideas and fresh approaches to come through. This often helps to solve the problem you were facing because by seeing things from a fresh perspective, you start finding different solutions and find that there is not only one way of doing things. There are many ways of doing things. It's a bit like thinking outside of the box. Sometimes we wouldn't have dreamed of doing something in a million years, and we find out that sometimes it just works. Life just flows, not from our control, but because we have let it go and let it be.

Forgive yourself

Sometimes you may find that it is easier to forgive others than to let yourself off the hook.

That is because we are naturally harder on ourselves. We put the pressure on ourselves and expect to do better. We are our own worst enemy. Not everything will go your way, and you can't be expected to do everything yourself.

Stop beating yourself up for what you can't do and focus on what you can do.

Do what is manageable for you. You are not a superhero, and you are not responsible for the whole world, despite people trying to blame you for it. This could be people from the media, friends, or even family.

If there are incidents that have happened in the past which you are not proud of, leave them where they are—in the past. Nothing you say or do can change what has happened before. It is over, and you thinking or feeling bad won't change what has happened. All you can do is learn from the event, apply what you have learnt to prevent it happening again, and move on. You have a lot to offer. So put it down to experience, and move on with your life.

You deserve to be the best you can be and that involves forgiving yourself from time to time. Forgiveness is part of loving, and if you truly love yourself, you will find it in your heart to love yourself no matter what. You will feel much better for it, and it will be a weight off your shoulders. This will give you the energy to spring forward with a real zest for life, empowered that you can move forward feeling good about yourself.

Forgive others, but never forget

I don't really believe that people forget things that have happened. Of course, they can forgive and choose, or shall I say decide, to not think about it again and start anew, but really they just push it to a different part of their mind.

It can be very refreshing if you are lucky enough to be able to do that, not everyone can. When you forgive someone, it is similar to a huge weight being lifted off your shoulders. In fact, you are actually doing yourself a favour and deciding not to take on the burden of another. The other party may not even realise that they have been forgiven, as you may have lost contact. However, you will feel a lot better for it and will be able to move on more positively with your life.

There are some people who forgive easily, but unfortunately, for one reason or another, the other party may do exactly the same thing again or hurt them in a different way. This is not very pleasant or fair. If this happens, it may be worth asking yourself what kind of signals are you giving out that they think it is okay to do that again? In life, you don't want to be perceived as a doormat to anyone, whether that's someone at your workplace, a friend, or a family member. Self-esteem is an important quality.

I used to let people walk all over me, until one day I decided enough was enough, I deserved better. Say it to yourself now. Once you have taken the step to see yourself differently, others will soon start following suit.

The decision part is easy; it's like a switch that you turn on mentally. However, your actual thought patterns may take a while as you have to form new habits. In a way, you have to reprogramme your mind to start thinking positively. You have been used to thinking a certain way about yourself, and now you have to retrain your brain to think differently. Try this exercise out for yourself and see if you notice the difference. Start by telling yourself at least three positive thoughts about yourself. It could be: 'I am beautiful, I am good at organising, and I am a very motivated person.' Then each time your mind starts disagreeing with this, simply repeat it to yourself, whether it's said out loud or in your mind. Soon, as the days go by, you will start to believe the statements you say about yourself. That way, if anyone tells you otherwise or discourages you, you know it's not true because you have reprogrammed your mind, so to speak, to know what you believe is true and what isn't.

You will get there; it may take a little perseverance, time, and a lot of love for yourself, but you will get there.

As a word of caution: I urge you to pay attention to the lessons you have learnt about the unpleasant incident. This is to help you avoid the situation reoccurring and also to protect you from similar episodes from other people. You should always protect yourself, especially after you have been hurt. After all, you love yourself, don't you? All too often, people are quick to protect others but forget about themselves. Things have a habit of happening to teach us a lesson. Learn from it and move on, but don't forget it because this is also part of the learning process.

Know yourself

Honour your values, and stay true to what you believe in. When you know yourself inside out and understand yourself completely, nothing can sway you or stand in your way, because you won't be influenced by what others say as you stand firm in your beliefs.

Sometimes this can be easier said than done, especially when people are discovering themselves and finding their own identities and own voices. Some people may imitate others for a while; this can include teenagers looking up to their idols or famous role models. They may do this by copying their trends or fashion styles, for example. This is harmless because, by doing this, they are still learning and finding out about what they do and don't like.

Call it a voyage of self-discovery, if you will, but this path can be discovered in many ways, and there is no one correct method of doing this

When you get to the point where you can honestly say, hand on your heart, that you know yourself completely, you have achieved a remarkable gift indeed. You have found yourself, and, therefore, you are not lost.

This is so important because the world is full of 'lost souls' and dreamers. This is usually the reason so many people want to 'travel' so that they can find themselves. Yes, sometimes travel can help, although I have also often heard people who have travelled around the world say that they realised that they had to return home to discover that what they were looking for was there the whole time.

If you want to travel in order to discover yourself, then do so. Do what you feel is right for you.

Be yourself

Once you have discovered who you really are, don't be afraid to show it. Show the world the real you. This is not the time to copy someone else because you have already found yourself. Be authentic. Don't be false, because that always has a habit of coming through.

You are wonderful exactly as you are, so embrace this beautiful you, and love yourself completely for it.

No one else can be 'you' like you can.

CHAPTER 7

SELF-CARE

When it comes to good health, it's so easy to take it for granted. You think this will always be the state your body and your good health, stamina, and looks will last forever, despite what other more mature women tell you. You simply don't believe it – in fact, you don't even hear it. Many times you just put it all down to jealousy or criticism.

Care for yourself

Loving and caring for yourself is vital to living a happy and healthy life. Sometimes you need to shut out the outside world and listen to what your mind and body are trying to tell you. Appreciate your body, and only put good food and drinks inside you. Your body is your vehicle, it requires and deserves the highest quality nutrients, which is fuel for your body. This, in turn, will help maintain and energise you.

Eat and drink healthily

Food is fuel for the body. So, giving yourself the highest quality fuel means that you will perform at optimal levels. You deserve to have the best of everything. Eating a balanced diet—including carbohydrates, protein, fats, fibre, vitamins, and minerals—will play a significant role in keeping you healthy and strong. Carbohydrates are good for energy, and these can be found in potatoes, bread, rice, and pasta. Fats also help provide energy. These can be found in butter, dairy spreads, and oils. Protein helps with growing and repairing muscles, bones, and skin and can be found in dairy products, meat, and eggs. Fresh fruit and vegetables are a good source of vitamins and minerals, which are great for keeping your body in tip-top condition in a number of ways, including boosting your immune system, helping wounds heal, repairing cells, and transforming food into energy. When you have a balanced diet, you are prepared both physically and mentally. You will find you are more alert and less sluggish when you eat the right foods, and food will help you perform at your highest potential because it acts as the 'fuel' to keep you going.

Keeping hydrated is also essential to performing at your best. Drinking plenty of water will help flush out all the bad toxins in your body and keep you hydrated. Try it for yourself. If you drink a glass of water in one go, you will instantly feel energised. It's a great pick-me-up to help you throughout your day. The body is made up of a large proportion of water, and we need water in order to survive. So make sure you drink plenty of it regularly to keep you refreshed, healthy, and alert. If you drink alcohol, it is a good idea to get into the habit of drinking a glass of water in-between your alcoholic drinks. This will prevent you from getting a severe hangover and keep you hydrated because alcohol is very dehydrating.

If you eat healthily and look after yourself, your body will thank you for it. Your skin, hair, and nails will also look great because the best food and drink is going inside your body. It should also result in fewer check-ups with the doctor because you will gain a boost to your immune system, which is always good news.

Show yourself some love, and eat and drink healthily. Your body deserves to be treated with respect, and you deserve to feel at your best and full of energy. It feels great to be healthy. Don't take good health for granted; look after yourself!

Exercise often

Get into the habit of maintaining your fitness now, as this will be harder if it is left until you are older. It is also a good way of learning discipline and perseverance

Exercise releases serotonin, which makes you feel happy and good about yourself. It helps to give you that 'can do' attitude and makes you feel like you can accomplish anything in the world. This also helps to keep you in a positive frame of mind, which is empowering and uplifting. When you move more, you can't help but feel good mentally, too. The benefits are rewarding and fun. Enjoy yourself while you do it; this will motivate you more and also enable you to maintain the habit of exercising regularly.

It won't be long before those around you will start to notice your newly found zest for life and ask you what has changed. Inspire them and encourage them to try it for themselves. Perhaps even ask them to join you. Not only will you reap the benefits, but so will others around you. It's human nature not to want to miss out on anything, and when those around you see the benefits that regular exercise brings to you, they will want to join in and experience this for themselves.

You will also find improvements to your hair,

skin, nails, body, posture, and mind as exercise enables oxygen to circulate all around your body.

Exercise will also teach you how to be disciplined, and, as your stamina improves, you will also learn about perseverance, a skill that is often required in everyday life. It is good for stress release, which is important and will help you to remain calm while others may be 'flapping' around you. Your sleep will also naturally improve, and you will find it easier to get to sleep and feel refreshed when you wake up.

Sleep matters

Sleep is so important for your health and well-being. It keeps you mentally alert and equips you so that you are ready for action during the day.

When you are young, you may not appreciate the effect it has, but as you get older, it can make all the difference between having a good day or a not-so-good day. You want to be at your best, so you can fulfil your potential. You want to give your optimal performance at all times.

This takes good habits and discipline. Make getting enough sleep part of your daily routine. Most people need at least eight hours of sleep to feel at their best. Some need less, and some require more. Get to know yourself so well that you can work out an average of the amount of sleep you need to be at your best the next day.

Sometimes a lack of sleep can't be helped. If you have sleepless nights often, this is usually a sign that something is troubling you. Lying awake won't help you come to a conclusion; instead, it could actually make it worse because you will have less sleep staying awake thinking about it. If this happens, you need to decide whether you want to write down your thoughts there and then, or try your best to get to sleep and put it out of your mind until the morning. There have been occasions when I have laid awake at night buzzing with ideas for articles to write or other creative endeavours. I decided to get up to write it all down, partly to get the idea out of my mind and also so I don't forget it. After I have done this, I usually find that I feel much better, almost as though a weight has been lifted off my mind, and this helps me to relax, which in turn helps me to fall asleep.

It is better to do yourself a favour and get some sleep; everything usually looks so much better in the morning. You may even find an answer to whatever was troubling you and be able to resolve it easily.

Lack of sleep can be very stressful not only for you but also for those around you. It isn't pleasant being around a grouchy person. You are not helping others by acting this way. Do something about it.

Learn about what calming activities you can do before you go to bed. Try and go to bed at a similar time every night. Perhaps read a book or have a relaxing bath before it's time for bed. Switch off your phone and other mobile devices so that you are not distracted. Your rest is more important than social media. You won't miss that much and can always catch up the next day. Make sure you create boundaries, and don't let people contact you throughout the night unless it truly is an emergency. You deserve to have peace of mind. Your body needs to regenerate so it can perform at its best the next day. Give it the best possible start.

Look after your skin

Start a beauty or daily skincare regime early on and try to keep this routine. This will serve you well in later years. Regardless if you are out partying or no matter how tired you are, at least remove your makeup (if you wear makeup) to remove any dirt and residue, before you go to sleep. Overnight the skin regenerates, and dead skin comes to the surface. This is why when you wash your face in the morning, you remove the dead skin cells, and pave the way for new cells to surface.

If you don't remove dirt and grime from your skin at least a couple times a day, you could get spots. Spots are formed when the pores are clogged. This has a lot to do with fluctuating hormones when you are young. Looking after your skin is a good habit to get into. You will feel the difference in your skin immediately, and it will make you feel good about yourself.

Beauty sleep is also essential for great-looking skin and so is drinking plenty of water, eating healthily, and taking regular exercise. It's great to have fun and eat and drink all kinds of things, but if you stop for a moment and take a look at the damage it does to your skin, it makes you wonder what it does inside your body. Your skin shows the tell-tale signs instantly of what happens if you don't look after yourself. No one else can do this for you. You have to take care of you. Yes, you inherit your skin, but maintenance of it is your responsibility.

Your skin is the largest organ of your body, so look after it, and you will soon notice the difference. When someone compliments your skin, it does wonders for your self-esteem.

Skin tends to dry out as you become older so it is important to start moisturising and looking after your skin while you are young. I know that this seems like a million miles away, but it can suddenly creep up before you realise it.

For instance, I used to have rather oily skin as a teenager and was prone to spots and blemishes. When people told me it's better to have oily skin and that it will stand you in good stead in the future, I didn't believe them. I couldn't see the benefit; I only saw the blemishes and how self-conscious they made me feel. I learnt from reading magazines how having a good skin regime can really help. So I cleansed, toned, and moisturised my skin every morning and night, exfoliated twice a week and applied a face mask once a week. My skin gradually became clearer. I also drank lots of water, slept well, ate a balanced diet, and exercised regularly. A combination of all these actions helped my skin, which in turn helped me start to feel better about my appearance.

Take care of your skin in the sun, too. You don't want to appear older than necessary. Wear sun cream if you are out in the sun, and protect your skin from the elements. You want your skin to look fresh and radiant, not old and haggard, so avoid this by taking care of it now. You will be amazed at the difference, and the good thing is that you can see the difference instantly by looking in the mirror.

Meditate

Learning to tune in to your feelings can be a discipline in itself. Meditation works for me. Even if it's just for 10 minutes a day, I find it clears my head of 'busy' thoughts, and I find I gain clarity and focus from it.

Contrary to popular belief, meditation can be attained from various forms of activities. To be in a meditative state basically means being at one with what you do and being blissfully attuned to the present moment. You are not thinking of anything else other than what you are doing.

The traditional approach is to sit with crossed legs and listen to either a guided meditation or music for a few minutes or a lot longer. Sometimes the hardest point is at the beginning when you have to train yourself to dim down the chatter inside your mind along with any distracting thoughts that pop into your head. I say 'dim down' because that is part of learning to control your thoughts and plays a role in becoming disciplined. For many of us, all we need to do is to get quiet for a few minutes each day and centre ourselves.

If you prefer to be 'doing' rather than simply 'being', then there are other activities that can help you reach a 'meditative' state of mind. For instance, gardening can be wonderful as it makes you feel at one with nature, and you can easily lose yourself in the flow, especially if you hear the birds are singing and you are blessed with peaceful surroundings. Painting, drawing, and sewing can also be very calming and relaxing. Anything that removes you mentally from your current situation can help. Some people prefer to go for a leisurely walk. Whatever you do, be sure to take some time to do this regularly.

Meditation can bring so many benefits to your overall health and well-being. It especially benefits the mind by helping you to maintain focus, clarity, and stay centred and calm in the knowledge that you can handle anything that comes your way. It is that inner strength that is the difference between perseverance or giving up and letting things happen to you. Try it and see. It may take practice and patience, but you'll never know if it can help until you try it for yourself.

Relax — take it easy

In this fast-paced world we live in, where everyone is used to rushing around with no time to spare, it is easy to forget what matters in life. We seldom take the time to just 'be' and enjoy moments. Now and again it is good to take time out of your normal routine and just be yourself. It can be quite refreshing to not have any particular place to go and to be in no hurry to do anything. It immediately takes us within ourselves. It is good for creation because a lot of creativity comes from inside. The most inspired actions are taken after someone has had a chance to just take it easy and go with the flow.

While there may be people who simply do not understand the concept, as they are just so busy 'doing' all the time, they probably find that they are the ones who are more stressed and may also find that they seem to be constantly chasing their tails. It is all very well being a busy-bee constantly, but it isn't productive if you do not achieve anything apart from being worn out and stressed. So remember to take some time out for you. It doesn't have to be for long, even a few minutes a day will make the world of difference.

Being relaxed once in a while is a beautiful thing, as it allows your mind to rest and your body to recharge its batteries. In fact, you will probably find that you are actually more productive in the long run. In some cases, you may come up with creative or inspiring ideas that you wouldn't have had if you didn't take that rest.

We are not machines or robots. Contrary to what you may have learnt in school, in your work place or from your loved ones, the human body is not designed to just go, go, go all the time. If that happens, it may cause a person to start running on empty and can even cause illness. At times this may occur so you have an excuse 'to rest'. There is no need to have an excuse. You know when you have had enough and cannot take any more. Do not wait until it is too late or you are in bad health or shape. Know yourself enough so that you can tell when to take it easy. Sometimes a slower pace is all you need to get going. That's why it's good to take a break or a holiday now and again. After a great holiday you will feel refreshed, recharged, and ready to go full steam ahead with a newfound joy for life.

It is not fair to snap at those around you because they do not necessarily know when you have had enough, so check in with yourself and go at a slower pace when it comes to that time.

CHAPTER 8

LAUGH AS OFTEN AS YOU CAN

Laugh often

Keep a sense of humour; it will help you through many upheavals and keep you from getting too low. It is a best-kept secret that many people use. It can be used to get out of an awkward or uncomfortable situation and ease a tense atmosphere.

Laughter is good for the soul and is ever so good for the mind. It releases endorphins and can also help keep you young and fresh looking.

Smiling is also good and can be infectious. Try it for yourself. When you smile at someone, it is very hard for them to refrain from smiling back at you. The world is a much brighter place when you smile, and it will instantly give you a lift no matter what mood you are in.

They say a good hearty laugh can be medicinal; it can also be therapeutic and a remedy for practically everything, as long as you don't laugh at someone else's expense.

Laughter and humour is a great way of making friends and building relationships. For instance, if you are about to enter a room with lots of people you have never met before, such as a networking event, and you feel awkward and uncomfortable about it, a good way of breaking the ice is to use humour. If you see someone else who looks equally uncomfortable, go over to them and introduce yourself even if it's to say, "I don't know about you, but I get really nervous at these events." Chances are the other person is just as nervous as you or perhaps even more so, and it's a great way of befriending another by admitting to your vulnerability. After all, we are all human.

Even if you laugh at something on TV, it can make a difference to your day and your outlook. If someone you know is feeling down, try and cheer them up or help them see the brighter side. Not only will this help them, but you will find that you will also feel better and glad that you could help. Laughter has a knock-on effect on those around you, which is very positive. You can change the atmosphere or room instantly when you make someone laugh or smile.

That is why there are so many comedians in the world. For instance, I love watching Michael McIntyre, a British comedian on the television, and it wasn't until I went to one of his shows and saw him live that I realised that I wasn't the only one who shared his sense of humour. There were thousands of people who did, and I saw for myself how he had a huge effect on a very large crowd.

Comedians want to make a positive impact and also to make a difference to someone's day or life. Everyone wants to be around happy, joyful people. They make good company and are easy to get along with. Humour is a universal language. It doesn't matter what language you speak, you can always understand humour and funny situations.

Keeping a sense of humour is essential. Even if you had an unhappy childhood, it can help to look upon the past with a sense of humour and lighten the burden, then you don't feel so bad.

I have done this many times. I recall a time when my mother was having a conversation with her brother, and they had had a few drinks, but for some reason, they kept forgetting what they said. They repeated the same conversation over and over again with the same surprised reaction from my mother each and every time. My sister and I were becoming more and more frustrated at hearing the exact same thing being said over and over again, and she became quite angry in the end. Now when I think back, I can't help but laugh, as it was very funny and it was one of those moments you could never capture again. Sadly, they are both no longer with us, but these memories live on. With so many serious issues in the world, it's good to make time for laughter.

CHAPTER 9

CONFIDENCE

Confidence can be learnt

People often believe that when it comes to confidence, you either have it or you don't. That's not necessarily the case. Unfortunately, many schoolteachers today give all their attention to the 'confident' child who is more demanding and louder than his or her peers. The rest of the class assume the same people will get the teacher's attention, so it doesn't matter what they do because it doesn't make any difference. This is sad and can be part of the root of the problem society has today. When there are lots of young adults feeling like they don't matter and that nothing they do makes a difference, they grow up with low self-esteem.

I can relate to this. Just because I was quiet, people assumed I was shy. I actually wasn't shy; in fact, I rather enjoyed the attention. This is probably why I wanted to be a famous pop star and be the centre of attention for a change. In my late teens, I somehow found that inner confidence within me. Perhaps it had to do with finding my own identity; I'm not sure, but I think having my own sense of style and fashion helped a lot. Then there was makeup, which meant I could be whoever I wanted to be. I loved to experiment with makeup and hair colours, like a typical female teenager, I suppose. There was something else: I had gumption. I had a relentless drive and energy that kept me going after what I wanted. Yes, perhaps I had tunnel vision, but so what? For far too long I had been standing in the shadows and blending into the background while others took the limelight. This time it was my turn to shine.

Of course music had a big impact on me. I looked up to pop stars like Madonna, Prince, and Cyndi Lauper, and I thought: 'If they can do it, then so can I.' I wrote hundreds of songs and played a couple of instruments, but I sang better, to be honest. I danced so much. I think dancing above all things helped my confidence to grow. I would normally be nervous before crowds, but when I danced, it was like the faces all disappeared and faded into the background while I danced. It was like my own little world.

I believe everyone has that something inside of

them that they love to do. Everyone can feel confident at some point in his or her life, whether they choose to feel that way in front of others or not. I discovered that confidence can be learnt and acquired with practice. It is like a light that you can turn on or off whenever you want to.

For instance, if you practice appearing confident, people will perceive you as being that way. Being around positive people will help; observe your confident friends and see what things they do. Some people use humour to help them and some learn more things and acquire more knowledge on subjects that the majority probably know little about.

Believe it or not, your posture and the way you stand and walk has a lot to do with how you feel about yourself, and it also affects how you appear to others. So stand tall with your shoulders back and walk like you are somebody. Be proud of who you are. If it helps, smile.

Dress to suit how you want to express yourself; this will instantly make you feel more confident. Speak like you mean what you say. Put energy and effort into all that you do; this will, in turn, help you get the best out of life.

If it helps, set a task you would like to do each day. This may be speaking to someone new, smiling, or just being friendly. When you have achieved something, give yourself a pat on the back. It is so important to reward yourself; this will help you build confidence as you feel good about yourself.

You have a right to let your light shine.
You have a right to be confident.

Do not worry if you don't feel confident now.

Don't worry about making mistakes

Mistakes are part of life and play a big part in how we learn. If we never made mistakes, we would never grow as individuals. Don't be afraid of falling. I remember when I was a child, my mother always used to tell my sister and I : "Look down, and watch where you are walking." She didn't want us to fall and hurt ourselves or step on any dog mess. Looking back, I can see how she was just being overprotective and caring in her own way, but as I grew older, I wish I were taught to look up and ahead more. That way I would appear more confident and proud, I wouldn't be afraid of falling, and maybe I would have taken more chances in life. Who knows? I hear many people have become successful by taking more chances and probably failing more times. They aren't afraid of pushing forward, regardless of mistakes they make, and if they fall, they get back up again and either choose to continue or try something else.

I find it useful to ask yourself: 'if something doesn't work out, what's the worst that could happen?' Yes, you may be embarrassed, but you will learn from the situation. From another perspective, why not ask yourself: 'What if it does work out?' Now that's a whole different way of looking at it.

Consistency is key

Doing something regularly is more likely to get you to where you want to be rather than if you do something now and again or when you remember. The more often you do something, the better you get at it. As they say, 'practice makes perfect.' This will inevitably have an effect on how confident you start to feel, and it may even soon start to feel like second nature to you.

An example of this is when I was first taught to get the ball in the hole in golf. At first I just couldn't do it. I practiced, and once I had learnt to focus on the centre of the ball and focus on the area behind it, I did it instantly, and I kept on doing it

This served me when I used to work in commercial banking. Every Friday afternoon the team used to get together and take turns putting the ball into the hole. One time they asked the ladies to join in.

Everyone was reluctant, and I had my head down as usual. They were surprised that I wanted to have a go, and I admit I did act quite innocent about it. To their surprise, I got the ball in the first go. The ladies cheered me on (as it was ladies vs. men), and the men really took it badly. They couldn't believe it and even asked me to do it again, which I did. Guess what? I got it in again. I then won the makeshift cup that week. There was one man in particular who took it very badly indeed as he had always won in previous weeks. This reiterated to me that practicing and doing things consistently can make all the difference. This boosted my confidence in that office.

New habits need to be done at least a few times before they are created. Naturally, it may seem hard at first. You may want to schedule it into your calendar or set an alarm as a gentle reminder to help you.

For instance, when starting a new fitness regime, doing it regularly and seeing it through all week or even for a month will make you feel so good about yourself and help you feel like you have achieved something. It will have a positive effect on your body and mind and is terrific motivation for you to continue. Others around you will also be inspired by your sense of commitment, and you may even inspire them to start a fitness routine of their own.

Balance is important

Do a little of everything, and you will feel much happier and fulfilled. This, in turn, will help you feel confident about yourself as you express yourself to others with a positive outlook. It shouldn't be all work or all play; a mixture of both is better for your mind, body, and spirit. Many times people get fixated and find it hard to see the wood for the trees. Give yourself permission to relax and have a little fun. It will do you the world of good, and when you return to the matter or task at hand, you will have a fresh perspective and may even feel inspired. Don't be worn down by the routines of life. You've heard the phrase 'life is short', and it is. I realise this only too well, particularly as my mother died when she was only 47 years old. When you have a parent who dies young, it has a tremendous effect on how you see life. It is always in the back of my mind each year when it is coming up to my birthday that I am getting closer to the age she was when she died. It really gives you something to think about.

So do things in moderation. It's okay to go out and have a good time; it is okay to stay in and read; it is also okay to do relaxing and creative hobbies. Just because someone else doesn't enjoy what you are doing, it doesn't mean you can't do it. Suggest to them to go and do what they enjoy and you do what you love and then perhaps you can meet up after. Life is too short to please others all the time. It is your life, and you only have one, so make sure you do the things that bring you joy, too. It's not always about other people; you deserve to have enjoyment in life, too.

Not everyone understands the concept of balance. I often think it's something that needs to be learnt. Working all the time can affect your soul and your heart if you let it.

Take control of your life while you still can. Think about what you enjoy doing. Ask yourself what makes you happy. Then think of things that need doing that may not fill you with joy, but are necessary (for instance, cooking and doing house-work). If the task is monotonous, try to make it as fun as possible if you can. Perhaps play some music while you do it or think of things to look forward to, like where you'd like to travel to, and make the experience a little more pleasant for yourself.

I tend to do activities every day that are good for my mind, body, and spirit. For instance, for my mind, I may do something creative, such as create a piece of art or read. For my body, I may do some form of exercise, and for my spirit, I may get quiet, pray, and meditate. I find this really helps me on a day-to-day basis, and if I am not feeling like myself on a particular day, I usually find that it's because I haven't done something in one area. For instance, if I don't get time to meditate or get some quiet time to myself, I get a little irritable and snappy.

Balance is the key to a happy life and doing a little of everything helps to maintain this; it keeps things flowing smoothly. If you get into this habit while you are young, it will stand you in good stead in the future, and you will be able to pass this on to others.

CHAPTER 10

BUILDING RELATIONSHIPS

Relationships

Relationships are a big part of everyday life, whether we like it or not. The world is made up of all kinds of relationships.

We cannot escape from it; wherever we turn and wherever we go, we will always be involved in some form of relationship. It is part of human nature and part of being in this world.

Some people may choose to isolate themselves from others, and some even say they prefer animals to humans. In reality, we are not supposed to be alone. We all need each other for a little company and to share knowledge, a joke, or a heartfelt gesture.

If we all got along well, the world would be a much happier and brighter place to live in. Unfortunately, it isn't always like that. Even neighbours squabble from time to time, and siblings quarrel over things that appear petty to others.

We have a choice: we can either make the effort or we can stay bitter and alone by choosing to remain angry and behave badly towards each other. It isn't a good disposition to be always grumbling about others, and jealousy is even less attractive, but that doesn't mean people aren't guilty of it. Look inside your heart, and I bet if you are honest enough, you can think back to a time when you were also guilty of having these feelings. I know I have, and I am quite ashamed of these moments, but guess what? I'm human, too. We all do it. It's human nature, but we can do something about it.

We can 'try' to be a better person. We can try to compromise or at least agree to disagree. Try it for yourself; the next time you find yourself about to fly into a rage at a neighbour or friend, count to 10, take a deep breath, and either reach a compromise or simply agree to disagree and move on.

I'm sure we would all like to live in a better place, and having nicer relationships is a good place to start.

Be approachable

Being approachable goes a long way. People are more inclined to tell you things and help you if they find you helpful and approachable. You should be genuine and not false when you convey your pleasantries and feelings with people. People can always tell if you are being false, and it isn't very nice. When you are nice to people, more often than not, it is a two-way feeling.

Yes, there will be days where you will feel a little 'grumpy', but don't let those moods darken your spirits in such a way that it affects others around you and spoil your day. Nobody likes a 'grumpy boots' so make a decision to get yourself out of that mood as soon as possible. I say decision because, most of the time, simply deciding to change your mood can dramatically help turn it around. Unless, of course, you have had some bad news, then it will obviously take longer.

For instance, when somebody asks you for directions, rather than see it as an inconvenience, see it as an opportunity to help someone out. We've all been lost before, and it can be stressful at times, especially if we have to be at a certain place by a specified time. Besides, you never know when you'll find yourself in a similar situation.

With all the stories and news we hear in the media, sometimes it may feel safer to be guarded and perhaps even a little defensive, but this won't help you in the long run. It may keep you from forming friendships and building relationships with others, which would be sad. No one wants to be alone all the time. While it's good to have your wits about you and be cautious, especially in this day and age, here's a reminder that it's also good to be friendly and generally liked for your endearing nature.

Many times approachability is linked to being flexible, which also helps. Being friendly and warm-hearted is part of being approachable, and a smile always helps, regardless of the situation.

Be likeable

Some people like to appear as though they are not bothered whether people like them or not. I say 'appear' because, in reality, it is usually what they crave most.

Everybody likes to be liked, perhaps some more than others, but I don't believe that people enjoy feeling left out. I think they build up their defences and pretend that they aren't bothered, when deep down inside they wonder why they are not included. They probably ask themselves: 'What's wrong with me?' I know that this is the initial feeling because it has happened to me many, many times in my life.

I recall asking a teacher when I was in the sixth form: "Why don't the other class members include me?" She was quite taken aback I felt that way and said that it wasn't so much that they wanted to exclude me, it's because I appear as though I don't need anyone else. She went on to say, "You're self-sufficient." This actually surprised me; I then explained that even I liked to be included and have friends. She still seemed rather taken aback. This proved to be quite a revelation for me, and I started to make more of an effort to join in conversations.

However, as I grew older and started my working life, I soon discovered that, although the majority of people were nice, there were also those who were just plain rude and spiteful. Funnily enough, this often came from the more 'mature' work colleagues, who really should know better and set a good example. I tried my best to get on with them, but they were just false and just liked to gossip about me behind my back, even when I was within hearing distance. Even after confronting them, they acted as though they didn't mean it that way but continued in their ways all the same, so I left them to it and tried to keep my distance as much as possible. These types of people are generally set in their ways, so there is no point in trying to persuade them. Simply agree to disagree, and continue to be pleasant. You are dignified after all.

It's true not everyone will like you just as you probably won't like everybody. Nobody's perfect. But you know what? That's okay. As long as you make the effort to be friendly and nice the majority of the time, there will generally be a good feeling around, and we all like to feel good.

Love

Love comes in all forms and, like relationships, it can be found in many bonds:

- Parent to a child. When a parent first sets their eyes on their newborn baby, they are naturally overwhelmed with emotions and instinctively feel a need to cherish and protect their child from everything bad. It is almost like falling in love in a way. As you connect and bond with your child, this bond is strengthened and is like no other experience.

- Husband to a wife. When you have met the right person whom you want to spend the rest of your life with, there is a strong connection where you want to get close and be almost a part of them. It isn't always something you can explain; it is more of a mutual feeling. You take an interest in each other's lives and want to make each other happy.

- Sibling to a sibling. Siblings naturally have a connection, and even if they don't get on, there is usually a protective and collective feeling that you belong together as you are from the same family unit.

- Family member to family member. Family members share the same ancestors and often similar interests, and they usually support each other in times of need.

- Friend to a friend. Friendship is a great gift indeed because you choose your friends. You often share similar interests, sense of humour and socialise a lot. Friends are also a source of comfort as well as joy.

- Owner to pet. Many pet owners treat their pets almost like their children in a way; it fulfils their nurturing side. They want to look after their pet while also keeping pets for companionship.

Love is a beautiful gift that evokes a multitude of good feelings. It involves kindness, patience, generosity, and good humour.

Sometimes people can get a little confused and mistake other feelings for love, such as anger, jealousy, obsession, and controlling behaviours. On the contrary, these feelings may disguise themselves as love, but they come from a very different energy. It can often be hard, particularly at the start of a romantic relationship, to differentiate love from jealousy because all too often the recipient gets showered with affection and attention, which they enjoy.

Usually, it isn't until it gets to a later stage where the person who is jealous starts to show his or her feelings and become angry towards others who give any attention to his or her object of desire. Often it isn't until the jealous person lashes out that they discover that all is not well and perhaps this isn't quite what they had in mind. Love should be a happy feeling, not full of fear.

For love is not about control; love is about giving freedom and wanting the other person to be happy and do things out of choice instead of feeling they have to do something to please that person. Love is about expansion and growth, not about feeling stifled or restricted.

Parents, in particular, may be overprotective and say this is because they love you so much. Without realising this, this could actually prevent the child from wanting to take risks in life and may even restrict them from 'flying' when the time is right. Yes, they mean well, but there needs to be an element of self-discovery in order for a person to grow and be themselves. The same goes for relationships. Oftentimes, one person in the relationship may feel threatened if the other person takes up a new hobby or a course to improve themselves. Having other interests is perfectly natural and is part of experiencing life. It doesn't matter if you have different interests, it could actually make conversations more interesting and your relationship more fulfilling, so there's no need to feel threatened by this.

Love is about all good things in life; it should bring you a sense of happiness and surround you with optimism. Love is what life is all about. Embrace it.

CHAPTER 11

COMMUNICATE

Communication

Communication plays a big part in everyday life. Many times, it is the reason why people have arguments or disagreements, and can often be avoided. The art of communication is such a useful skill to have, which we often do not realise when we are young.

One thing we don't take into account is that communication is a two-way thing. We should not just blame the other party, which so often happens. We are also responsible for our own actions and that includes verbal as well as physical actions. When we speak or write, we should do so clearly and it should be intended for the other person to grasp the concept easily without having to struggle or guess what the other person is trying to say or what they mean. Be prepared; like any skill sometimes this may take practice.

Speak from your heart and learn how to express how you are feeling. For instance, ensure your body language and eyes are aligned with what you are saying. Look at the person when you are speaking to him or her and face towards them to show you are interested in what they are saying. Use their name, if you know it, when you speak to them, as this attracts their attention and will help with building and developing relationships. This also applies to family, friends, colleagues, or someone you are in a relationship with as well as other people you meet.

Express Yourself

Most arguments stem from a lack of communication, whether it's from someone forgetting to tell someone something or perhaps not making it clear. What one person assumes is understandable may not necessarily be clear to another. The art of expression can go a long way towards building a stable relationship.

By the same token, when one person thinks the other hasn't been open with them, they may start to doubt what they say and the actions they take. This can often happen in romantic relationships and if left unchecked, could lead to all kinds of problems in the future. In order to prevent this from happening, it is better to be as clear as you can in a diplomatic way, and if you think the other person hasn't fully understood, you may wish to double-check with them to confirm.

For instance, you may have made arrangements to meet friends for dinner, and although you have mentioned it to your spouse or partner and they nodded their head at the time, it is worth clarifying with them again nearer the time just to be sure, in case they were just going along with what you were saying at the time for a quiet life. This way, there is no danger of crossing wires or instances where you didn't tell them or didn't realise you meant this weekend. As long as you don't say it in a condescending or patronising way, you should be fine.

It's when people make assumptions that problems occur. An example of this is when one person assumes that you are both going to stay at their parents' home for Christmas this year instead of your parents. It is better to discuss this early on in order to avoid any unnecessary disagreements or bad feelings. Just try and be as transparent as you can to avoid this situation arising. If it is too late for this, then try your best to resolve it as early as possible because you don't want it to turn into a bigger issue than it already is.

Miscommunication doesn't just happen in

romantic relationships; it happens in families a lot, especially if feelings are hurt and others are more sensitive than you think. It could be you that it's happened to. If that's the case, try and resolve it in a calm manner and look at it for what it is: a mistake. Look at it with a little love and compassion. Particularly with families, you don't want it to escalate into a feud. You are family after all. Practise the art of communicating. It's the key to a peaceful life.

CHAPTER 12

BE PRESENT

Live in the present

I have seen it all too often: a person keeps talking about the past. They say how good everything was in their day, and this would never have happened in their time. You know the ones; I bet you can think of someone right now. They often include the word 'remember' in the sentence and tend to drift off to some place far away in their mind.

This is when a person is not present. They are thinking of the past. This is very common in more mature adults; they think of happy times when they could do more and when they had a lot of fun. In a way, this makes them feel good about themselves. Yet again, they can feel so nostalgic that it hurts them. It hurts because they realise they can't do anything about it anymore. Everything has changed, and the people in their memory may not even be alive now.

This can be so sad to witness, especially when you see how the joy in their eyes turn to tears of sadness.

Having regrets can be terribly sad; it can come in different forms: from regretting not asking someone out for a date and therefore never knowing what could have been to not realising a dream you have always wanted to do. It could even be something that you have been meaning to do, but just haven't had the time or haven't gotten around to doing it. If this is the case, my advice would be to make the time.

I remember my mother suggesting that I record the stories that my grandmother, whom I was very close to, used to tell me. I remember saying, "Yes, as soon as I get the chance, I'll do it." My grandmother lived in Mauritius so I suppose the chances were quite minimal. But guess what? I never did get around to it, and my grandmother passed away. Her stories were left untold all because I didn't get around to it. I could go on endlessly saying, "if only I...", but, to be honest, that's not going to change anything. Instead, I have to learn from this valuable lesson and pass it on to others, so I'm passing it on to you in the hope that you don't make the same painful mistakes I did.

You see if you have your attention fully in the present, you don't have time for regrets. Today you are making tomorrow's memories, and that is worth remembering.

Only thinking and planning for the future is also just as bad because, although it may appear optimistic, in reality, you are so busy focusing on the future that you are not enjoying the moments of today.

Remember you will never get this time again, and that is certainly something worth thinking about. Live in the present, enjoy the moment, listen to the sounds, smell the air, and pay attention to what is happening all around you. When you get accustomed to doing this, you will feel so much more fulfilled with a wonderful sense of well-being. You will also be much better company to have around, as no one wants to be around someone who is elsewhere mentally. Attention can be a wonderful thing. Enjoy the moment.

Put your heart into it

No matter what you are doing, try your best to do it with your whole heart. Put everything you have got into it. Not only will you enjoy it more, but you will be adding a little of your essence into it and that is truly a remarkable thing.

You see, it's easy to do things half-heartedly and without much effort; anyone can do that. But when you put a little finesse and style into it, you will find no one can do it like you can. This goes for any task you can imagine: from menial tasks, like doing the laundry, typing a letter, or creating a painting. Even if you have never done something before, have a little respect for yourself and make your own mark on it. Have your own take on things.

This way even the most laborious tasks can seem somewhat pleasurable. For instance, if you hate ironing but love listening to music, play loud music and sing to your heart's content while you iron. Not only will you get it done faster, but you may not even want the task to end because you are enjoying yourself so much. (Now there's a thought! Who would have thought ironing could actually turn out to be fun?)

If you are working for an employer and you dislike your job, try going to work and putting your all into it. Do it to the best of your ability, and take pride in what you deliver. This will soon shine through, and who knows? You may even start getting praised for your work, and, get this, you may even start to enjoy it.

People can tell when you do things half-heartedly. It has a habit of coming through, no matter how much you try to hide it. If you can't change things completely overnight, such as a job, then start by changing how you approach it. If you begin by altering how you think about things (for instance, try watching motivational videos or listening to positive and inspiring podcasts), this will eventually have a knock-on effect on your actions, which will then bring about changes elsewhere in your life.

As you become more self-aware and conscious of your thoughts and actions, this will inevitably have an effect on all other areas of your life, including your relationships with loved ones.

People can tell if your words and actions don't match and if you are not aligned mentally and physically. For example, if you are not fully present and your thoughts are elsewhere while you are having lunch with someone, you may think you are fooling the person in front of you, but you are just fooling yourself. Showing others the respect they deserve is also respecting yourself. Give yourself the best chance in life, and do everything wholeheartedly. Who knows? You may even surprise yourself.

Be mindful

Be aware of what you do; this includes your thoughts as well as your actions.

This not only gives your thoughts more power and energy, but when you do things purposefully, you are in control and that in itself can be empowering.

When we leave decisions to others and have no control, that's when panic or doubts can set in. We can even become a little anxious because we haven't instigated the event. We cannot control everything, but, to a certain extent, we can control our thoughts and the way we view things. In order to create a positive environment, it is essential to be able to first control our thoughts. For thoughts eventually turn into words.

Words are also very powerful, so be aware of what you say and how you say it. For instance, saying things one way could bring joy and saying it another can bring altogether a very different outcome. So think before you speak; be aware of what you are saying. Consider if what you say will benefit others or whether it will be demotivating.

Be at one with your thoughts, and learn to train them to be most effective so that they benefit you instead of bringing you down. Your internal voice should uplift and encourage you and not put you down. When you are mindful, you become aware of what your mind generally thinks about things, and you can train it accordingly.

Keep a clear conscience

When you have a clear conscience, you sleep better, you are more at ease, and everything flows better.

You do not need to worry unnecessarily about work or other issues. You are mentally free. You don't want to burden yourself with things that could have been avoided.

Do things with an open heart, and always be aware of what you do. For instance, if you think something is questionable, don't do it. It's as simple as that. Why would you want to put yourself through unnecessary stress and problems? No matter what pressure you are under, whether it is financial or peer pressure, nothing is worth losing sleep over. Worrying doesn't change anything; it is very exhausting and will wear you down mentally as well as physically if you let it.

When you worry, you feel anxious and often go over things in your head again and again. I would suggest you try and do things that take you out of your head. For example, exercise is a great way of getting out of your head because it means you have to be physical. Another example would be to do something for someone else so that your focus is on them and not on you. If this doesn't work, try getting quiet for a few minutes, close your eyes, and listen to your breathing and nothing else; focus on your breath and just be still in the moment. You can do this to relaxing music if you wish. In that moment of stillness, become aware that there is nothing you need right now apart from listening to your breath. If you prefer to say a prayer instead, then do so, for this also creates a similar feeling. As you take the worry from your shoulders, take a deep breath before you open your eyes. Afterwards, you will be enveloped in calmness, you may feel differently about things, and things won't feel quite as bad.

Take your time

Patience is a virtue; having patience can help resolve so many situations and can also help you grow as a person.

There's no need to rush everything. You have all the time in the world to experience life fully. Obviously, this may all go out the window if you are working for someone or if you have a deadline to meet, but apart from that, try and be at ease with yourself and accept that everything has a time and place for things to happen.

It is human nature to want things right now, especially as we are programmed to think fast and act fast due to commercialism in a fast-paced world. Don't let that affect your judgement or your decision-making. I often find that if you feel pressured to make a decision there and then, it is usually a warning sign not to go ahead. If you find yourself in this situation, go with your gut or instinct and do what feels right. If you are attuned to your inner feelings, you will usually make the decision that's right for you.

A quick technique to do this is to mentally focus on your lower abdomen area. Imagine there's a heavy weight or a ball there. Do this for a minute, and you will feel aligned with your beliefs and how you feel about things, despite the environment around you. It is a grounding technique that helps you to feel at ease and also works as a short confidence-booster if you are about to go in front of a large audience. Life is to be treasured, not rushed.

CHAPTER 13

YOUR GIFTS

You are talented

You are talented and have gifts. Everyone has talents, and some choose to keep them hidden. It could be because they are shy or lack the confidence. It could also be that they worry what people will think of them or whether people will laugh at them. If you keep your talent hidden for most of your life, that could lead to that awful word: 'regret'. Nobody wants that.

I admit I have been guilty of this. When I was a child and a teenager, I had a vision to sing, write songs, and become a pop star. Nothing else seemed to matter to me. I would spend evenings singing and practising dance routines along to my records. I was determined, despite my mother telling me how I was "building castles in the sky". I didn't care; I just continued writing songs. I got as far as taking regular singing lessons, for which I had to audition. Yes, I had a lovely singing voice and still do, but the saddest thing is that I didn't do anything with it. Although, I had the drive and determination, I lacked the self-confidence to sing in front of crowds. I just couldn't do it. I could sing in front of one or two people, but that was it.

Yes, you have many talents, but if you keep them hidden, they may turn into regrets, and there is nothing more sad than that.

Follow your vision

Once you have decided what you want to achieve in life, go for it!

Make the decision, feel it within your heart, and use your head to make it happen. Don't look to others for advice and ask their opinions; this is your vision, not theirs, for they have their own dream to chase, which may be quite different from yours. Others close to you, including close friends and family, may try to dissuade you.

We only have one life, so make it yours and make your dreams come true. Research, plan, and find out exactly what you need to do and what steps will need to be taken in order to get you closer to your vision. The internet is a great tool for researching ideas, stories, plans, and exact steps. Read as much as you can about your chosen field or subject; this will come easily to you if you are passionate and have a hunger for making your dreams into reality. If possible, talk to people who have achieved what you want to do. Keep an open mind, and have a willingness to learn. Don't assume you know it all before you even begin the process. Learn from others' mistakes, and take on board what needs to be done. After you have learnt what steps you need to undertake on a practical level, the next part is having the courage to make it happen. You can do this!

Have determination and discipline

Drive and determination tend to go hand in hand; it is the spirit within you that keeps you moving forward.

Determination is having the right, positive mindset and the physical energy to carry out your disciplined efforts. Passion for what you do can also be part of this because it will help drive you forward.

Have a plan of action to help you; realise that this will take discipline to see this through. Consistency is the key to success. When you are disciplined and follow regular habits, this helps you to maintain the momentum you require to succeed in what you want to achieve.

Being disciplined will help strengthen your mind and keep you on track, especially when things or people try to distract you.

One way of becoming more disciplined can be as simple as getting up an hour earlier each day. At first, it may seem almost impossible, but after a few days, you will start to get into the rhythm of it, and it will soon become a new habit.

You may not even realise how easy it can be to make this part of your daily routine, yet it can make a tremendous impact on your productivity. You don't even have to do a lot in that first hour. Even just spending some quiet time, gathering your thoughts, and perhaps jotting down a maximum of three things you want to accomplish that day will help. It is similar to setting your intention. The three things don't necessarily have to be big things. In fact, it could be a step towards completing a task on another day. For instance, if you are planning on writing a blog article, this could be made up of a number of steps instead of one big step, which may seem overwhelming.

First, you may want to research a blog idea. Then you will want to find your target audience and then design a photo. Another step could be to research keywords to include in your article, and eventually you will sit down and write the blog article on a separate day, feeling much calmer and more prepared. It may seem like a long process, but if you are feeling overwhelmed and lack inspiration, these little steps will soon add up. If you are consistent with them, they will lead you to move forward with your plan in leaps and bounds as you gain momentum in what you do.

Having determination and discipline are a winning combination.

Stay positive: Stay focused

Try and keep a positive outlook. There are times when this won't be easy, especially when those around you are being particularly negative. Try not to let it affect you too much. When you are positive, everything good is possible.

Try and stay focused on your goal by visualising the outcome you want. When things look bad, keep thinking of the outcome no matter what. This will keep you going when things look bleak, and it will also remind you of your dream or goal. Try and get into the habit of doing what I call a success exercise regularly for at least five or ten minutes.

For example, play some calming, relaxing music in the background. Sit up or lay down. Start by taking a deep breath in, slowly breathe out through your mouth, and then proceed. Imagine yourself unwinding from your head to your toes gradually. It may help to imagine a white or golden light flowing down your body as you sink deeper into relaxation. Picture your successful life in your mind. Describe it in detail. Use your senses to help you.

If you are looking for success, imagine yourself being successful. What does it 'feel' like? You may be picking up an award for an achievement. Include all the details. Make it as real as possible.

Then, start to count up to five slowly as you make a small movement with your feet and work upwards towards your hands, shoulders, and neck. Then open your eyes, and take a deep breath in and then a deep breath out. You are now ready to continue with your day.

Doing this exercise regularly, at least once a week, will help you to stay positive and more focused.

Do what you love

Don't just do what's expected of you. That is someone else's dream. You are here to live your life, not someone else's. Parents and guardians may mean well, but at the end of the day, it is your life; you only have one, so live it the way you want to.

I recall someone who did just that. I went to an

all-girls school from the age of 11, and I knew a girl from school who used to get ridiculed rather a lot. Other girls openly told her she was thick and silly. She was always in the lowest classes for subjects. To be honest, I found her very friendly and upbeat, despite all the stick she got frequently. I admired her in a way because she wanted to be a doctor. She would tell everyone about this with a smile on her face. She was very confident that she would achieve her ambition, despite people laughing at her and saying she wasn't brainy enough. She continued anyway. I bumped into her many, many years later, and she immediately came up to me as friendly as ever. Guess what? She became a fully-qualified doctor. She fulfilled her ambition, despite what others said. So while they were in low-paying jobs, complaining about their lives, she became a highly-paid doctor doing what she loved and what she always wanted to do.

Discover what you'd love to do, and go and do it, no matter what others say. You owe it to yourself to love what you do.

Follow your passion

It will keep you going when times are tough.

When you have a flame in your heart for something you love doing, if you encourage it and help it to grow, it will soon become a fire. Once you feel the fire in your heart over something, you know that this is your passion.

It may take a while for you to discover your true passion in life. Don't feel pressured into finding what you are meant to do. It may even happen while you are doing something completely different. Many people discover their passion after starting a hobby. You never know when it will happen. It doesn't have to happen while you are at university or college. You will know it when it happens because many times it doesn't feel like work; you are eager to get up in the morning and get on with it. You may even lay awake at night bursting with ideas about it and feel excited about life. It doesn't have to be that way though; some people may be much calmer and have a more relaxed approach to their passion, more of an inner glow rather than a blazing fire. All that matters is that you are aware of it.

People with passion are seldom deterred from their dream. They may listen to the advice and opinions of others, but, to be fair, most of the time they choose to ignore it, which isn't always good. They may have tunnel vision or be single-minded, as I was.

I recall working in a department store, which

sold predominantly clothes. At the time, I looked after the children's wear section. I remember one afternoon, as I was conscientiously folding sweatshirts on the shelf in a corner, the manager came up to me and asked how I was doing. She was kind-natured; she always had a smile on her face, and she was very confident. She said I was doing a great job and while what I was doing was beautiful, she advised I looked up from time to time and see the rest of the department. The rest of the department looked presentable and laid out, but the point she was making was that I had a habit of becoming so engrossed at the task at hand that I often didn't stop to take a look at the bigger picture. I was quite shocked about this actually and learnt a lot about myself that afternoon. It was as if I had my shades removed, and I could really see things for what they were. Excuse the pun, but this changed my whole perspective on life, I assume this had an effect on my work because I then was asked to look after the front of the store and ladies' fashion, which I excelled at and enjoyed every moment of, especially when I was selected to go to buyer's meetings to choose the next season's collection. That one comment had such a profound impact. I was no longer the teenager in the back of the store folding sweatshirts; I was now the 'front of house' person. The assistant manager even noticed that I walked differently when I came to work. I had a new zest for life, which I applied to every area of my life.

So I have to say, sometimes it is also a good idea to look at the bigger picture.

That way, you will see how everything you do affects someone else, and that kind of teamwork can help. For example, when we go to a restaurant, we are often oblivious to the process of preparing and serving our meals because we are generally supposed to have a relaxing atmosphere where we can switch off from our normal routine. We wouldn't be aware, for instance, of how the waiter takes our order and how he or she passes it to the kitchen, where it goes to the chef. The chef has the pressure of preparing all the meals at the table by a certain time so that the guests at that table can eat together. The chef relays orders to the kitchen staff, and they are each allocated different tasks to do in order to prepare the different meals. After the meals have been prepared, they are placed on an area for the waiters to collect, and the waiters are informed of this so they can serve them to the allocated table, so we can eat at our leisure. Every member of staff in that restaurant affects each other. If one member makes a mistake, it has a knock-on effect and may result in a complaint if not managed well.

By the same token, what you do affects others. We all need others from time to time. It is often said that teamwork can make a dream work, so it's better to be aware of those around you while you follow your passion. You never know, they may even be able to help you along the way.

CHAPTER 14

SHARE

Share your gifts

You have probably heard this many times before, but it always better to share than to keep things all to yourself. This doesn't mean you can't keep anything to yourself. Obviously, if someone has told you something in confidence that they would rather not share with others, then don't share it. It's just that now and again it is good to share your gifts.

You may say that you are not ready or that nobody would want to listen to you, but how do you know that for sure unless you try? Sometimes we say we are not ready when really we are just afraid—afraid of putting ourselves out there or afraid of ridicule or being humiliated. This fear can stop you from fulfilling your dreams and prevent others from appreciating your talents if you let it.

I say 'if you let it' because it is still like giving

yourself permission in a way. I have made excuses for not pursuing the career that I initially wanted. As I mentioned before, I originally wanted to be a singer/songwriter and although I practiced, wrote songs, and went to singing lessons, which I had to travel three hours for every Saturday afternoon, it wasn't enough. It wasn't enough quite simply because I was afraid that people wouldn't like my voice if I sang in front of a large crowd. I lacked confidence in that way, and so despite all the hard work I put in and the dreams I had in my head, it all went unnoticed. I blamed so many things and so many people for this, including my parents, it quite simply didn't happen because I let it slip by out of fear.

It's taken me many years to admit this. The hardest part was to admit it to myself and then to those around me. This is why I'm telling you today. Don't let fear or excuses stop you from sharing your gifts. You have been given a particular gift for a reason and to keep it hidden would be a shame.

Share your love

Love is for sharing; it's as simple as that. It is something that we all need. Nobody is an exception; that includes you. No matter what type of upbringing you may have had, everybody wants to be loved.

Some may pretend they don't and appear cold. Usually, it's because something has happened in their life that has hardened them. It is unfortunate, but people often keep others at a distance in order to protect themselves, especially if they have been hurt in the past. It is a natural instinct, and can keep a person from finding love, if they choose to let it. You may be one of these people. If so, all I can say is that time really is a great healer and no matter what someone else may tell you, no one can get you out of that thought pattern but yourself. It is almost like a grieving process that needs to be accepted and gone through to be able to come out the other end and be able to feel love once again.

Love is a gift in itself; I should really say it is 'the' gift because if you do things without love, it comes across as false and you may as well not give it. When an action or gift is done through love, you can feel the sincerity of it wholeheartedly, and it will lift the spirits of the recipient and also the giver.

When you do something out of love, you can't help but feel good about yourself, and, in a way, this good feeling can be infectious. For example, if you give someone an unexpected gift, as a heartfelt gesture, more often than not the other person starts to feel all warm and fuzzy inside, especially if he or she is taken by surprise. It evokes all good feelings for them, which they naturally pours out into the world as displays of emotion, such as kindness and warmth. The same goes for love. I don't mean just romantic love; I mean any form of love. Love is necessary in the world, and as we all need it, let's continue to make it a happier place to live in.

Share your joy

A sense of humour is a truly remarkable gift. It can make almost every situation feel so much better. It is like sunshine after rain and can feel like a breath of fresh air.

Some people don't even realise that it is a gift. They assume everyone has it. Not everyone shares the same sense of humour, but a little humour goes a long way. It has certainly helped me in my deepest, darkest, and most troubled times of my life. Just when you think you hit rock bottom, along comes humour to hold a torch over your situation and light it up in such a way that it totally transforms what you are thinking and the way in which you see things. It is good like that.

Have you ever been in a situation where you are not supposed to laugh and make noise, and the more you become aware that you are 'not supposed to laugh', the more you start giggling? I remember when I was 17 and my friend and I took a trip to The National Gallery in London. We were both studying art and really enjoyed it. The security guard kept 'shushing' us, and the more he did it, you guessed it, the more we laughed. In fact, it got to the point where we were laughing uncontrollably and just couldn't stop, and the more we tried to stop, the louder we got. Eventually we got asked to leave that particular area, and it was such a relief to get all that laughter out of our system when we were outside.

It is good to laugh and express joy. It is good for your soul, your heart, your mind, and generally good for your health.

Joy lifts your spirits and can help spur you on to reach your highest potential with ease. It is great for relationships of all kinds. Embrace your humour; it is your unique gift to the world

Share your knowledge

Knowledge can be a powerful tool. It can be used for enhancement or destruction; you have the choice.

Education is made up of knowledge of different subjects, but it is in not the only way of obtaining knowledge. There are many people who have left school and, despite not being hugely successful

in school, have gone on to have rich and rewarding careers.

With the internet today, knowledge is readily
available at a click of a button. Gone are the days
when children may have been too nervous or shy to
question their teachers. Now they can find out things
for themselves and become more self-sufficient.

Having said this, you do not have to remain
alone in your pursuit of knowledge. There are many
forums and groups either in the form of clubs or
over the internet that integrate people with similar
interests. Learning can be fun, and learning within
a group can be even more enjoyable as you all share
common interests, exchange stories and bounce ideas
off each other.

From another perspective, it is always good
to learn from each other and help each other. For
example, learning from another's mistakes could save
you a lot of time, effort, and even money. Likewise,
just as you learn from others, it is nice to also share
your own knowledge. You may not think you know
a lot about a particular subject, but when you start
talking about it, you may be surprised at the extent
of your knowledge. There are a variety of ways to
share your wisdom: you could write a blog filled
with tips and advice, you could answer questions

on social media and forums, you could teach, and you could help people if they are stuck with something at school, work, college, university, the shops, the hairdresser's, or wherever you are. I bet there are situations that occur every day where you can find opportunities to help and add value to someone's life if you stop and think about it.

I remember when I was at a supermarket years ago, and I wanted to whiten some curtains. I was renting at the time and so wasn't that wise about household products. I was standing reading the back of about three different boxes, and a lady (not a staff member) came up to me and said which one she would choose. Then another lady came and advised me of what she would do. It was quite funny; before I knew it, I was surrounded by a small crowd of wise women who advised me about washing instructions and everything else to do with whitening curtains. It made my life a lot easier, and I learnt a couple of things I didn't know. As well as learning how to whiten curtains, I also learnt that it's good to be helpful, and if you can help someone out in a small way, by sharing your experience or even a little knowledge with them, it could make all the difference. You never know when you are going to need to 'pick someone's brains'.

After all, a little knowledge goes a long way.

Share your message

Sometimes you may feel that you have nothing to say and can't think of anything that may add value to someone's life or be part of a conversation. At these times, it is worth remembering that it's okay to be quiet at times, as these are the moments when we gather our thoughts. Our thoughts are with us no matter what the situation or however many people there are around us.

But that doesn't necessarily mean we do not have a message to share. What you may think is trivial to you could make a great deal of difference to someone else's life. It could not only help them, but it could transform the way he or she thinks about things to such an extent that they are able to completely turn their life and world around for the better.

Someone is waiting to hear your message; they need your help and guidance. They are waiting for your story; you may not realise it and may come up with every excuse you can think of to try and avoid sharing your message, but if you don't, you may be kept from helping someone who really needs to hear it. Many of us want to make a difference in the world or in someone's life. This is your opportunity to make that difference, to tell your story, and to share that message. You may think no one is interested and nobody will care, but are you really willing to take the risk of not helping that person? It could be a young person or an older person; it doesn't matter. What matters is that we all have a responsibility in some way to help each other.

This will take courage, and you may not have the confidence right now. If this is the case, try and recall a time when you were at your lowest point, felt that you were completely alone, and had no one to turn to. How did you feel? I'm sure that you wouldn't want someone else going through that. I'm sure that you would want to help them, if only in a small way. Reach out to that person who needs you and is waiting to hear what you have to say.

Share your time wisely

Time is the greatest gift you can give someone. It is precious, and, unlike a physical gift, once it has been given, it can never be taken back.

Be particular about who you spend your time with and what you spend your time doing. It is easy to pick up bad habits from those around you. When you surround yourself with people who have a positive frame of mind, this will have a positive influence on you, and this, in turn, will help you to influence others around you in a positive way, too.

You don't have to be by yourself all the time; just be aware of the behaviour and mindset of others, and be conscious of how you spend your time.

Time management is a big topic in today's society. In school, we are trained to divide our day into blocks of time, which separate the lessons throughout the day. When we're older, it may become easy to forget and spend time doing more of one thing than the other. This shouldn't matter too much as long as we have balance. We should do the things we love and allocate time to be productive and creative if we choose to. Yes, the majority of people spend a lot of their time working, but it's what we do with our leisure time that can sometimes hold the key to our entire well-being.

For instance, it is all too easy to spend a lot of time watching TV. Some people can quite happily sit around watching one box set after another. If that is what makes them happy, then that is up to them as long as they are aware that they may not accomplish what they set out to do that day. In other words, as long as they don't start taking it out on others because they fall behind in their tasks, that is their choice.

If you want to try out time management for

yourself, I would suggest you start out by writing down a list of what your priorities are for that day. It only needs to be a couple of tasks. Then below these, write down the actions you need to take in order to achieve these tasks. This is probably best divided up into half-hour slots.

For instance, if you know you need to complete an assignment, write it down as a priority. Then list how you will achieve this. For example, you would probably first need to research your material. Then you may want to create graphics or graphs and then write down the main points you want to make. Finally, you fill in the missing parts and write it down in full. By doing this task in smaller chunks, it makes it more manageable for you and it won't feel so overwhelming. Even if you only complete a couple of steps, at least you know you are on your way to completing that assignment.

If something doesn't get done, don't beat yourself up over it. Simply move it to the next day. You may soon start seeing a pattern emerging; that way you will discover how most of your time is spent.

I also think it's important to write down your achievements at the end of the day. This will leave you feeling good about yourself, and it will also encourage you to continue your success. Time is a gift.

CHAPTER 15

ALL THINGS MONEY

Manage your money

Money is a necessity in life. Once you learn how to manage your money, you will feel in control and organised, and you will actually have peace of mind and clarity over your finances. There is no need to go to bed worrying about it. Once you learn about money, you can manage it.

To be honest, I didn't really learn about money properly until I was in my 20s and then again in more detail in my 30s when I had to because I became an account manager in a bank. Soon I learnt the art of money and found myself showing others how to manage their accounts on a daily basis. Many were scared, even those who were in high-paying careers were petrified when it came to even looking at their accounts, let alone managing them. They preferred to bury their heads and worry about it later.

You are smart because you are taking control of what governs everyday society: money. You heard the saying, 'money talks'. What you have to remember is that money is a commodity and needs to be controlled and moved to where it needs to be. From a holistic or spiritual perspective, money is considered to be a form of energy. In a way that makes sense, you exchange money regularly for goods or services as part of everyday life.

In basic terms, you need to have a budget. Don't be scared; a budget doesn't necessarily mean you have to limit your lifestyle. As a matter of fact, it actually gives you more freedom because you can spend a certain amount each month without feeling guilty. Knowing you won't be overdrawn or need to borrow from others will help you to feel better about yourself and help you sleep at night.

Basically, make 2 columns: write income in one column and your outgoings in another. When you get paid, write that in your income column. Here is an example:

INCOME	OUTGOINGS
2000	Rent 1000 1st
	Gas 60 4th
	Water 40 8th
	Total: 1100

Write down all your bills in the outgoings column. I also like to put the date they are due to go out of my account beside them to make my life easier. Then total this up.

Subtract this total figure away from your income figure, and that is what you have for the rest of the month.

INCOME	OUTGOINGS
2000	Rent 1000 1st
1100 – (total outgoings)	Gas 60 4th
900 left for the month	Water 40 8th
	Total: 1100

At this stage, it is a good idea to subtract another figure for your savings and transfer this amount to your savings account. That way you can build up savings, too.

Every time you spend, subtract what you have spent from the figure you have left over for the month. Remember you need to budget for the rest of the month so don't go crazy.

This takes practice and discipline, so give yourself a few months to adjust. After this, the process will become easier, and you will soon discover that you actually have more in your bank account than you thought.

As a tip, it is worth ensuring all your direct debits are scheduled to go out a couple of days after your payday and on the same day each month. Ask your bank how to set this up. When you write down your outgoings, make sure you include your food, going out, hobbies, birthdays, etc.

The good news is that after your savings have built up, you can splash out and treat yourself. This is a great incentive to continue your money habit.

Track your money

This goes hand in hand with managing your money. Write down every time money comes to you, whether it's in your account or not and when it goes out. Do not throw away your receipts until you have written it down.

This is imperative if you want to stay on top of your accounts and in control of your spending. It will also give you a boost and help to lift your spirits.

By keeping organised, you form a pattern and routine so in time it will become second nature to you. At first, it may seem like a chore and somewhat laborious, but once you get into your own rhythm, it will flow naturally. It can also be empowering because you know exactly where you are and this will have an impact on other areas of your life in a positive way. You will start to feel self-assured, and you will stand secure in the knowledge that you have got this under control, which you have because if you see that you are spending in one area, you can reduce it or reduce it from another area. It will also teach you to budget, which will benefit you and actually give you more freedom and goodies in the long run. Hey, you may even begin to encourage others to do the same.

Take control of your debt

Only borrow when you really, really need to. If you do, try and pay as much off as possible as quickly as possible to avoid high interest rates. Think positively;

imagine seeing your credit card bill or loan balance at 0.00. I used to do this, and it worked very well for me. Don't get stressed; the fact that you know what you owe and how much to pay is a good starting point. Now you can do something about it. If you get a lump sum, save some of it. Spend some, and put some towards getting your debt down. If you are truly stuck, get some advice. Do not get another loan or another credit card no matter how nice the person at the bank is and how much they try to persuade you. Keep picturing your debt balance at zero. Stay focused at all times. Imagine what you would feel like if you completely cleared your debt. What would you spend your extra money on? How would you reward yourself? Come on, you've got this. I believe in you. Start now, and you will be debt -free sooner.

Get into the habit of saving

As soon as you start earning, it is a good idea to save at least 10% of your income in a separate account. If you organise with your bank to set up a monthly standing order, this will be automated and you won't even have to think about this. Try and set it up around the date you get paid. This will make it easy for you.

Before realising it, you will have built yourself a little or large nest egg, which you can either choose to spend or put towards a larger goal, such as a car, holiday, or house. Getting into this habit while you're young means you won't have to rely on others as much. You will become more self-sufficient and in control of your finances.

It may seem difficult at first, but after you have done this a couple of times, it gets easier and you won't even notice it. When you see how much money can accumulate, you will feel good about yourself and your achievement, and you will reap the benefit when you treat yourself.

There are many different banks and building societies around; look for a bank that suits your needs and lifestyle and ask as many questions as you require about the types of products and services they offer. Ideally, it is a good idea to have three types of savings accounts. One you have instant access to should you require it, one for mid-long term savings like a holiday or a home, and another where you don't have any access to it until many years later, such as a pension or a five-year investment. It is up to you whether you are prepared to take low or high risks on the long-term investment. Most people prefer to have a bit of both, but I would recommend getting financial advice before you commit. Oh, and as a word of warning, always remember to read the small print.

My experience in retail and commercial banking has definitely taught me that. Do not sign anything without reading the small print, no matter how nice the person presenting it is to you.

Saving is easy when you know how; don't make it more complicated than it needs to be. If you can't put a certain amount in, put in a smaller amount. The main thing is that you get into the habit of saving. You will be so glad you did.

Know your money

This may sound strange, but it's a good idea to find out as much as you can about all aspects of money as soon as you can. After all, it is the one thing that is used to exchange value throughout the world. I have always said, 'The more you learn, the more you earn.'

But that doesn't mean money only goes to those who are blessed with a good education. Even if you left school and didn't get many qualifications or didn't go to university, you still have a chance to learn about how you can manage money and how it can benefit you. It is in your best interest. You have to depend on yourself, especially when it comes to money. I learnt or, should I say, had to learn from a young age that you can't depend on anyone else for money. It isn't anyone else's responsibility but yours.

It's not your parents' responsibility to bail you out if you have money problems, and it isn't your responsibility to bail your parents or other people out. Don't carry that weight on your shoulders. Life can be challenging enough without carrying additional 'baggage' around.

If you feel it is scary and you don't know where to begin, start as people used to do in the days before the internet: start by picking up a book. It doesn't have to be a complicated book; Just pick up a straightforward book or research online for advice and tips. Nowadays you can find so much information if you look for it.

This will take time and effort, but it will serve you well in the long run. You are educating yourself on money and building a better and more secure future for yourself and your loved ones. It's never too late or too early to do this by the way. So don't use that as an excuse. The sooner you start, the sooner you can reap the financial rewards, which I am sure you will enjoy. Don't feel pressured when you are learning about your money. It isn't really anyone else's business. It's yours.

Learn about compound interest. In basic terms, this is when you leave money in an account and you acquire interest. If you leave this money in your account for a long time, you will accumulate interest on top of the original interest – this is known as compound interest. I discovered a useful book called *The Wealth Chef* by Ann Wilson. Ann talks about compound interest in the book and shares advice on how to invest your money for your future.

Find out where is best to put your money by researching on the internet how interest rates work and what are the benefits of having a credit card and by reading financial books. You could also find out about your credit score and how it works. Don't be disheartened if you don't have a good credit score; it can always improve. Mine did, and I have helped many, many others improve their credit score, too. It isn't the end of the world. You can improve your finances. When you educate yourself, everything will fall into place and make sense. It is also wise to shop around while you are researching for great deals on your utility bills, phone bills, interest rates, and other bills you have. You will be surprised as to what a difference this will make. It could be the difference between you going on that holiday or buying that outfit you want or not.

You are worth the time and effort it takes to learn about money, and once you acquire this knowledge and skill, nobody can take that away from you.

CHAPTER 16

DO NOT LIMIT YOURSELF

Fear is limiting

One of the worst things you can do that will block your creativity is to limit yourself. Many times it is because you start listening to others and are, therefore, taking on their beliefs about themselves, which is all too often because they choose to play small and stay in their own comfort zones. They can say it under the guise of looking out for you or protecting you, but it is really all about fear.

The fear they have really is about themselves. Sadly, these people are usually very vocal about their opinions and think they know better than anyone.

This can be easier said than done, but try not to let their opinions affect you. If you start listening to them, it will stall you and may even deter you from being who and doing what you want in life. By all means, listen to them if you have to, but don't let them control your thoughts to the point that you start to doubt yourself. Smile, acknowledge them, and thank them for their point of view. Then remind yourself of all the good things that are happening. If it helps, look over your list of good things about yourself and look over your achievements. If you have mislaid the list, then create another. This will remind you of who you are, the qualities you have, and the good you bring to others. It will also reiterate your self-worth and how you contribute to the world. You are on your path for a reason, and we all have a message to share with the world. Whether it's large or small, every contribution matters. You matter!

If someone tries to bring you down while you are growing, it is better to build an invisible bubble while they say their remarks so it doesn't deter your growth. Even if this is a loved one, just because they are close to you, doesn't mean they are immune to a little jealousy, and they are probably worried that you will leave them as you spread your wings. Not everyone can take and accept success from others. It's a difficult lesson to learn, but sometimes people prefer to keep you where you are and even where they can control you; this is often due to their own inadequacies and weaknesses.

There is such a thing which is referred to as 'the inner critic' that you may hear when you look to step out of your comfort zone. It is basically your doubt challenging you.

We all have this; it is a method of self-preservation that derived from a primitive era, back in the 'hunter-gatherer' times. It is like a defence mechanism that kicks in if we suddenly hear the sound of a predator or animal nearby that we think may attack or be a threat to us. It is a similar feeling to your hair standing on end. And is there to warn us and protect us, which is actually very helpful.

It is that voice that will ask if you are sure you are doing the right thing, if you are qualified enough, and if you should be going after your dream. It is the voice that often asks, if this is a good idea. It is doing this out of fear and also out of protection, and is a primal instinct, which we all have inside of us. The trick is to acknowledge it and learn to dim it down so it doesn't keep you frozen in such a way that you never want to do anything new, which may include stepping out of your comfort zone. There is no use trying to fight it because it is an extension of ourselves and, in a way, helps us to survive. We simply must learn to live with it and even show gratitude towards it, and then we choose to move forward in a way that is reassuring and kind. For instance, you could say either in your mind or aloud, 'Thank you for your concern, and I know you are looking out for my best interests. I understand that you are doing this out of love, but it's going to be okay; I've got this.'

Stop limiting yourself or letting others dictate to you. This could be as simple as someone saying that you shouldn't watch a certain TV programme, go to a certain place or country, eat certain foods, or do things a certain number of times. It is your life, and, quite frankly, no one has the right to tell you what to do. As long as you are not breaking the law, then it is up to you what you choose to do with your time and how you should spend it.

You have a right to make your own choices in life, and as long as it doesn't harm you or anyone else, then go and live your life the way you want to. Live your life.

Be flexible

Life can be unpredictable, and sometimes things may not go according to plan. This is why it is important to be flexible. If you are too rigid, this will limit you and could hurt you deeply. Don't make your schedule so rigid that you do not allow for the unexpected. Be willing to see both sides of the coin, and be open-minded to other people's opinions, feelings, ideas, and opportunities. You never know, the idea you least expected to work may prove better for you in the long run. There is no reason to be stubborn just for the sake of it. Listening to others may turn out to be invaluable.

Move forward

We often hesitate before moving forward. This could be for a variety of reasons, including taking a look around to gauge where we are, checking if we are mentally as well as physically prepared, wondering what others will think of us or about the idea we are about to undertake, or simply pausing for breath.

The important thing is not to stay paralysed in this moment and think too much about it because this may prevent you from taking the chance of a lifetime.

I have often found that sometimes it is best just to jump with both feet first into a situation. Yes, this may involve risks, but by doing this, you avoid over-thinking and getting nervous about something to the point where you won't take any action at all.

Nerves and anxiety can play a big part for us to find and make excuses for not doing something in life. Fear can be your worst enemy if you let it, or it can help you if you look at it in a different way. However you are feeling, it is worth remembering that everything is temporary. When you realise this, it can suddenly take a lot of pressure off you, and you will discover that suddenly things aren't as bad as you first thought.

It can also help to put things in perspective. For instance, by comparing your life to events going on in the world, such as third world matters, you may find that you actually have nothing to worry about. It doesn't matter if things don't go as well as you had hoped or planned because you can always do something different or have another go, depending on what it is.

So take a deep breath, and put one foot in front of the other. That is always a good place to start, and soon you will find that no matter what you do, you can't help but continue to move forward.

Expand your horizons

Step out of your comfort zone once in a while. This will do you a world of good, and you may even discover a side of you that you didn't even realise. As well as discovering hidden talents in you, it will bring a sense of excitement to your life. It will get your adrenaline going and put a spring in your step.

Stepping out of your usual routine may seem daunting and could even be the last thing you want to do, but if you don't do this, you will start to stagnate when you could be growing. It is good to give yourself a challenge or a goal now and again; it will help you push past the fear factors and embrace change. For example, I remember being afraid of horses, but I had always wanted to ride. So, after researching local stables, I picked up the phone and booked a lesson. I explained that I was really nervous, and they said not to worry. On the day of the lesson, I was physically shaking and didn't know why I was putting myself through it.

When I got on the horse, I must have passed my nerves on to the horse. It started fidgeting and even raised one of its back legs to scratch itself, which almost threw me off balance. Luckily, my instructor was very patient and kind, and she just started chatting to me as she led me to the field. Eventually, we chatted and laughed so much that I completely forgot about my nerves. Guess what? I got my balance. In fact, I did so well that I even rode hands-free at one point. I felt so good; so much so that I didn't want the lesson to end. It was a complete contrast to how I felt before the lesson. Afterwards, I felt like I was on cloud nine; I was proud of myself because I achieved so much just by stepping out of my comfort zone. It gave me a new lease on life, and I walked with a newfound confidence.

Growing is part of everyday life; it can also be enriching and fulfilling. Try to be the best you can be. Being the best version of you is so rewarding and uplifting. Try it for yourself and see.

I have to say, from experience, it is always best if it comes from you personally wanting to do this. If you only do things because others are telling you to or pushing you to, it won't work. Instead, it will feel like pressure, which in itself can have a negative impact.

To be the best you can be, you need to have the urge and the courage to do this. It has to come from you. Only you can make this happen for yourself and for the greater good of those around you. Have you ever thought that you may inspire someone else to take action? Yes, you.

When others see what you do, it makes them look at themselves and also question what they do. You may encourage others to achieve their dreams or goals without even realising it.

If you don't step out of your comfort zone now and again, you will never know just how good you could be. Now there's a thought: imagine not realising your potential just because you were afraid, scared, or lacked the confidence or courage to do it.

Be daring every now and again; do something you have never done before. It doesn't have to be something really dramatic. It could be as straightforward as planning a trip away or taking up a hobby you have always wanted to do. Perhaps you have always wanted to learn a new language or another skill, such as ballroom dancing or playing the harp. Whatever floats your boat and gets you excited. Go with it!

Doing something that you wouldn't normally do can be fun and exhilarating; it can make you feel alive and remind you that there is so much that life has to offer. There's no reason why you have to continue doing the same things over and over again. Yes, you can have a routine, as it is good for the mind to have some sort of discipline, but life doesn't have to be mundane unless you make it so.

DARE TO BE DIFFERENT.
DARE TO BE YOU.

It's your choice; you can choose to make your life as mediocre or as exciting as you like. You call the shots, and you control the boundaries. Even when you live by someone else's rules, no one has control over your mind but you. So, choose wisely and live a life that lights you up. Now and again, make your own rules and alter your own boundaries. Follow your own terms and conditions, and take control. You will be so glad you did. Put your own spin on things and make it yours. No one can do it like you can.

Don't pretend

Don't pretend to be something or someone you are not for the sake of others. In doing this, you are limiting your own abilities and talents in order to try and fit in with those around you. Yes, there may be times where you feel it is appropriate to just go along with what others expect you to do and be. This can be anything from trying to please your boss or impress a potential boyfriend or girlfriend.

However, overall, it is better to be yourself rather than trying to be something or someone you are not just to please somebody.

Don't sell yourself short. Your heart will tell you when you find yourself doing this because it simply won't feel right. All too often people go along with others for a 'quiet' life. This can be detrimental to your heart and to your soul in the long run. It is far better to be authentic and stay true to yourself than to be the person or do the things they want you to do. You may be able to pull this off in the short term, but these things have a habit of coming out, whether you want them to or not. You can't hide it. It may even show up when you least expect it to. Being false has a negative impact on yourself and those around you. People will respect you more when they know the real you and what you stand for. They may not like it at first, but then grow to admire these qualities in you, and they may even wish they had these qualities and had the courage to stand up for their own convictions.

Actually, I would go as far as to say that it is rather selfish if a spouse expects you to do the things they enjoy and you detest. They should know and love the real you, not try and manipulate you into being like all the others. After all, wasn't that part of the reason why they fell in love with you in the first place?

By the same token, don't pretend to be something you're not. All too often, people try to please others by portraying an image that they think will impress them. But, in reality, this is far from the truth. Be yourself.

CHAPTER 17

ENCOURAGING SUCCESS

Be grateful

Express gratitude for all the good things in your life. Not only will this encourage more good things to come to you, it will also make you feel good about yourself. When you start seeing all the positive things that are happening in your life, the future will appear brighter and you will have fewer worries.

Saying 'thank you' means a lot to people; it shows you value what they do for you and that you care about their heartfelt intentions. When someone gives you a gift, instead of saying 'Oh, you shouldn't have', try saying 'Thank you'. It will change the feeling of it and will confirm to the other person that you accept the gift graciously. Both parties have a positive feeling, and this has a ripple effect.

Take a few minutes each day to think about what you are grateful for that day. This will help you to see your day in a different light and focus on the positive.

Celebrate your successes

One way of being grateful is to remember to celebrate your success. Make it a habit to celebrate your victories in life, no matter how small. This will help you to feel good about yourself and give you the motivation to continue and attract more success into your life.

It will also help others around you as they may become inspired by what you do, which in turn encourages them to take positive action. It is very motivating to watch people succeed. It creates an air of optimism and hope for the future. Life is full of possibilities, and progress is part of this.

When you see that you are having a positive impact on the world, it fills you with a sense of well-being and a sense of pride. Sometimes pride has its benefits; it doesn't have to be a bad thing. When you take pride in a piece of work you have completed or something you have created and are happy with its presentation, it brings joy, not only to yourself, but to others. No one can take that from you. It is so important to feel good about yourself, and doing something rewarding can be instrumental in making this happen.

When others see you celebrating your success, they want to become a part of it. Remember, nobody likes to think they are missing out, and, at times, this will spur them on to bring about their own successes and start celebrating theirs, too.

Success attracts success. Go ahead and make it happen. Start by visualising, setting your goals by writing them down, planning the steps towards making them happen, and putting the work in consistently. When you have achieved what you have set out to do, enjoy it!

Treat yourself

It's okay to treat yourself occasionally. Reward yourself, especially after you have been working towards a goal that you have achieved. You deserve to treat yourself, and you don't require permission from others to treat yourself. Do not feel guilty about it. You deserve it. Everyone deserves a boost now and again; it helps you keep going and motivates you. When you reward yourself by doing something you enjoy or buying something you value, you feel good about yourself and feel a sense of accomplishment. This is good for your heart, your mind, and your soul.

It doesn't have to be a large treat like a holiday or a car; it could be as simple as buying yourself a cup of coffee or a bunch of flowers. When you have a treat, it sets a precedent that you value what you do and that you respect yourself enough to realise your worth. When you respect yourself, you will find that others start showing you more respect and may even begin to see you in a different light.

It is also a form of encouragement. When you have a good feeling, it triggers something inside that makes you want more of this feeling again, and, therefore, you are more likely to take other steps in achieving something so you are able to find a reason to treat yourself again.

Encourage others

Try and encourage others as much as possible, whether it is giving them a pick-me-up or cheering them up. There are many sad or demotivated people around: some are just lost and need guidance, some are lonely, or some are simply afraid and unsure of what to do or where to turn. It makes all the difference to know that someone is cheering them on or giving them advice or guidance in some way. While you may be self-motivated, don't expect everyone else to be. I must admit that is something I had to learn myself. I have always been blessed with the ability to be self-sufficient and self-motivated, and I naturally assumed that everyone is inclined to be this way. However, I now realise that not everyone is like this.

There is no right or wrong to this. We all need help from time to time, and you should never be ashamed of this. You don't know what is going on in that other person's life, so whenever you can, you should help them out as much as possible. You also never know when you may require assistance from someone else.

Having said that, this shouldn't be the only reason to help someone. Never expect to get something back after you have given. When you give, it should be sincerely and from the heart; otherwise, there's no point in giving in the first place. For instance, a smile costs nothing and that alone can be encouraging to someone. I remember when I worked in a department store and an elderly lady walked in. I greeted her with a smile and said 'hello', and she told me that I was the only person who had spoken to her all week. She thanked me for making her feel good about herself before she left the store. I have to admit I was quite taken aback at the thought of having nobody to speak to all week; it certainly made me think.

A smile can go a long way towards brightening up someone's day and helping people to feel good not only about themselves but about life and about the world. That one smile can change everything. So whenever you can, share your smile.

Pay a compliment

We all like receiving compliments; it can make you smile and can be like sunshine on a cloudy day. As well as accepting compliments, it is also good to give them once in a while. Giving genuine compliments not only makes the person receiving it feel good, it can also make you feel like you have made a difference, however small, and you too will get a warm, fuzzy feeling. Compliments also cost nothing, but they can make all the difference if they are said sincerely without asking for anything in return.

Sometimes people take others for granted, especially in relationships, and forget that people like to be complimented, too. It doesn't just have to be in relationships. A complete stranger can pay someone a compliment, even if they are of the same sex. It doesn't matter. Look for the good things about people, and you will probably notice more good things in the world.

See every day as a blessing

There are lots of people around who are quick to point out what is wrong in their lives; sometimes they just want to get things off their chest and unload their issues onto others. Some, however, seem to always feel this way and are often found complaining about everything and everyone. These are people to avoid if you possibly can. For instance, If you bump into someone like this, perhaps show a little empathy, smile sweetly, give them some reassurance, and wish them well before going about your day. These people have a tendency to bring others down with them; they may not even be aware that they have this effect on people. Don't be one of these people. If you find that you have similar traits, you can change these. It all starts with a decision. Simply decide you want to be more optimistic about life and start behaving that way. If you find it hard, try 'acting' that way, and, before you know it, you will have gotten into the habit of doing so.

You see, every action or behaviour comes from a decision to behave that way. We do not just happen to be a certain way. Sure, we learn or pick up habits and behaviours from our parents and those around us, but we can always choose if we want to proceed with a behavioural pattern or not. You have a choice, and, therefore, you are in control of your actions and also your thoughts.

Try getting into the habit of being aware of

and being grateful for your blessings. If you put this into practice, you will soon start seeing the world in a positive light and will hopefully inspire others to do likewise. For instance, when you wake up in the morning, think of or say three things that you are grateful for. It could be that you are grateful for being able to open your eyes, for being alive, and for waking up in a beautiful place, or for having a lovely family or significant other. If you start this habit early on in the morning, you will soon be smiling and be cheerful in your approach. It will get to the point where you can't help but smile. Others will see you in a new light and will probably ask you about what has brought about this change. Tell them. Who knows? You may help them in a big way, including changing their lives dramatically.

When you start seeing things differently, you will soon start finding that more positive things will begin to happen in your life, which in turn means you will have more things to be grateful for. What a fantastic way to be? So start counting your blessings.

CHAPTER 18

YES, YOU CAN

You can do It

I can almost hear my mother's words in my head. Whenever I said, "but I can't...", she would reply back, "There's no such word as can't".

When you get an opportunity to do something and you feel you are not prepared, it is quite natural to have doubts come into your head. It's when we start to let these doubts take over, in such a way that we allow it to paralyse us to the point that we decide not to take any action, that it is a problem.

When this happens, it is best to acknowledge that this is perfectly natural. Then basically reassure this feeling that you've got this, and you will go for this opportunity and take the risk. You never know, you may even surprise yourself.

In order to overcome these fears, you need to develop a positive frame of mind. This will help to put things in perspective and talk down to the negative self-talk. We all have negative moments and even negative days, but we have to put it into perspective and control it. If we don't, we will limit ourselves and will be unable to move forward with our lives in a positive way. Keep telling yourself you can do it, and push through those doubts and fears. When you do, you will feel exhilarated and may even achieve a sense of accomplishment, which in turn, will lead to you being brave enough to try other new things and feeling even better about yourself.

You don't know what you are capable of until you try so keep telling yourself, 'I can do it', and you will!

Believe in yourself

Self-belief is so important. It helps you by having inner strength in your abilities. Having a strong mind gives you a solid foundation to face any obstacles that may come. It builds character and self-esteem. You have no reason to doubt what you believe in. Stand firm in the knowledge that you know who you are. You know your values, strengths, abilities, and capabilities. Do not look to others for reassurance. You don't need anyone's permission to go for opportunities. Believe in yourself.

Get back up

There may be times when things don't work out the way you expect. You need to brush yourself off and get back up. This builds resilience, which is a skill that needs to be developed. Yes, there will be risks in life, but if you don't take them, you will never know what could be.

You may be familiar with the concept that it is not the number of knocks that you have taken which matters, but how you deal with them. In other words, it is the getting back up and moving forward, regardless of what has happened, that matters. Keep focusing on moving forward and the outcome you wish to achieve. If you focus on things going wrong, they have a habit of doing so, and usually the bad things keep occurring. In fact, stop focusing on the negative and instead put your attention on what could go right. This will make a big difference to your outcome. Try it for yourself and see.

There have been many times where I have taken knocks. For instance, when I couldn't use my right hand after a gardening accident, I was no longer able to work at a school, which I adored. I admit at the time I probably did spend some time wallowing in self-pity. It is perfectly natural to do this, but this action should only be short-lived. If it isn't, that is when serious problems arise. After dealing with the emotional side of things (i.e crying and letting my feelings out to anyone who would listen), I started being practical and planning what I needed to do to get out of the situation and kept taking these steps until things changed. The steps don't have to be significantly large, even small steps taken consistently will help make the shift and will help you to move forward. However, nothing would have changed if the steps hadn't been taken first.

So roll up your sleeves, and prepare to take control of your life. Don't let the knocks get you down.

Be persistent

'If at first you don't succeed, try, try, and try again.' You may have heard a phrase similar to this said to you at some time or another or may have heard it said to others. Whatever your thoughts are on this phrase and whether you agree with it or not, at some point in your life, you will have the opportunity to try this out for yourself.

The opportunity may occur at a time you least expect, and when it does happen, be prepared to experience feelings of frustration and doubts. Don't give up.

Giving up can feel like relief because it is the easy way out and sometimes may be the only way out, but before you take this into serious consideration, give it your best shot.

Why? Well, because you owe it to yourself. It is as simple as that. Just because something isn't easy, doesn't mean it can't be done, and just because something doesn't happen straightaway, doesn't mean it won't. Be realistic; some things just take a little more time than you had imagined. Remember patience often goes hand in hand with persistence.

When you develop the skill of persistence, you will also develop your character and your self-worth. Be a person of quality and integrity. Be someone you are proud to be. This will remind you of all the good you are contributing and discourage you from giving up when you are feeling down. Be the person who can hold their head up when they walk. Yes, I'm talking about being you. Be willing to put in the extra effort and go the extra mile if you need to. More often than not, you will be so glad you did. If you find it's not for you, then at least you have discovered this for yourself. You didn't give up or run at the first hurdle. A little persistence can go a long way.

Perfection never comes

It's easy to make excuses by saying you are not ready or you are waiting for the right time (when you have more money, better health, lost some weight, have more time, or after you have completed that course). No matter how many times you tell yourself and others that this is true, at the bottom of your heart, you know that these are just excuses.

This could be for many situations: getting married, travelling, embarking on a course, or starting a new career. It could even apply to asking someone you are keen on out on a date.

It's true you may not be ready, but you know being 'ready' may not actually ever come. You may procrastinate and want to wait for everything to be perfect, but guess what? There really is no such thing as perfect.

Perfection is a state of mind created so that we have something to strive for. The media and film-makers use this concept all the time, particularly in Hollywood films where the leading characters have perfect skin, teeth, and hair. Indeed, they may look perfect to the person watching the film. I can assure you, after speaking to many actors, that this is far from reality. If you get up close enough, it is often a completely different scenario altogether. In the harsh daylight of reality, you find it's not as glamorous, and perfection is farther away than they would have you believe.

That's not to say you shouldn't strive to be your best, look your best, or feel the best that you can be. You should always set high standards, that way you will feel motivated, bring value to others, and be of help to those around you, particularly your loved ones.

You can spend your whole life waiting until you are 'ready', and that could turn into regret if you let it. Don't let it happen to you. Act now before it's too late. Do it while you still have passion for it.

CHAPTER 19

LIVING THE DREAM

Dream big

Allow yourself to indulge in daydreams. I say 'allow' because you really have to give yourself permission to do the things you love. It is similar to when you were younger and you had to ask permission from your parent or caregiver before playing outside or doing something else. When you give yourself permission as an adult, you feel a sense of relief and are happy to skip forward and follow your dreams. It's not really that we require permission, but somehow we feel better when we receive confirmation from someone else that it's okay to do something.

If you don't dream big, you won't have anything to aim for and you will be strolling along your path casually, when you could be full of energy and really going for what you want.

Many times we find it easier to blame others and

use them as an excuse for not going after our dreams. Indeed, many of us do this without even realising it. We may blame our parents, our friends, our boss, or even our children. But you know what? If you are honest with yourself, the main reason you haven't followed your dream yet is not because of responsibilities, money, or your circumstances. This may come as a surprise, but the main reason you haven't followed your dream is because of you.

This may be hard to admit and you may not want to, but the sooner you admit it, the sooner you accept it and do something about it.

I have mentioned not limiting yourself before and the same applies for your dreams. You can dream as big as you like, so why would you choose to limit yourself and your dreams?

When you have a dream, visualise what you would like to achieve and see yourself living the way you want. Really absorb it into your being with all your senses, your heart, and your soul. Then begin planning your strategy. These are the first steps between dreaming and turning your dream into reality.

Almost every success story started with a dream. What will yours be? Whatever you choose, make sure it is something you love and will make you sincerely happy. If you are going to dream, you may as well dream as big as you can.

Your dream

To live the way you really want and to have your dream lifestyle, you must first have a vision in mind. Every goal starts with a vision or an idea. You need to be able to picture it in your head first and then take the necessary steps to turn your dream into a reality.

It doesn't matter how small it starts; many ideas have been written on sticky notes or on the back of a piece of paper. Inspiration can pop up anytime and anywhere. It can occur while you are out with your friends, in the bath, or while you are shopping. It is common to get sudden ideas in the middle of the night while you are asleep or in the midway stage between alertness and slumber. Catch my drift?

I have many ideas at around three in the morning. I get these so often that I now have a pen and writing pad in my bedroom so I can quickly scribble these down. Don't rely on your memory because these moments of inspiration have a habit of being forgotten if left long enough. Trust me, I've been there.

Make the most of these insightful times. I am sure that these gifts have been given so we can do something with them. If we don't, you can count on someone else getting the same or a similar idea and acting upon it. How would you feel seeing someone do something with the idea you thought was yours? Not good, I bet. These gifts have a habit, if not used, to pop over into someone else's mind to get used there.

After you have your idea or vision, be clear with what you want to achieve. This is the first step toward achieving your dream. Clarity goes a long way. The rest of the steps are merely all about you taking a series of actions to prepare you for your dream.

Believe

Once you have something in mind, believe that you can achieve it. When you believe in something wholeheartedly, you will find yourself undeterred from your actions and achievements. You will be unshakable and that will mean you will be unstoppable on your path to achieving what you have set out to do.

When you believe in yourself and your pursuit of your dreams, it will enable you to become immune to any negativity that may surround you. When people criticise you or your dream, it will bounce right off you and may even bring a smile to your face. I have often found that criticism from others often occurs when they feel threatened by what you are doing, as it often shows them up in some way. It is almost like bringing a magnifying glass to examine where they are in life, and this often results in them lashing out in defence because it makes them look small or mediocre.

It is wise to acknowledge and possibly even thank them for their concerns, but don't dwell on their comments too long. Remain strong and positive, focusing on your own dream and on your own vision.

It takes courage, determination, and energy in pursuing your dream so put all your energy in the right direction – on your dream. It will help you in the long run.

Most of all, believe in your intention and in what you do, and do it with integrity. Have your own take on things.

Act 'as if'

This may sound pretentious or false, but acting as though you are already living your dream goes a long way towards achieving it.

It sends out all the right signals to others, and also when you 'feel' as though it is real, it almost always has a way of becoming reality. It is just a matter of time.

Many people who are living out their dream life-style have often acted 'as if' before they reach their goals. If you enjoy these thoughts for even a few minutes a day, you will probably feel different, and despite being in somewhat different surroundings, the fact that you have imagined your dream means you can go there anytime you want reassurance that you are on the right track. I bet it will make a difference to you. Try it for yourself and see.

It doesn't matter if the lifestyle you have imagined is a complete contrast to your current one. Every goal that has been achieved first started out as an idea. A single thought can go a long way. Never underestimate the power of your mind. The mind can control how we feel and react to everyday things, and it can also be instrumental in helping you achieve what you want to in life.

Practice having a positive and productive mindset, not a destructive one, which will not help you or others around you. Aim to preserve your mind and maintain its strength. That way you won't be easily swayed or manipulated by others in life because you will know your own mind.

Once you have practised acting 'as if' a few times, others may remark on little changes in you. Your posture may be different as you may hold and carry yourself better. You may stand taller and appear generally more optimistic and more positive to others. This is because you will now have an idea of which way you are heading and what direction you wish to take. Once you know where you are going, you will feel far more self-assured. It will probably help with your peace of mind too. Just think, this is all because you made a decision to go for your dreams in a big way.

CHAPTER 20

PERSEVERANCE

Persevere

There will be times when you feel like giving up on something. This could be because it seems too difficult, like it's never going to happen, or perhaps things are not working out the way you thought they would.

In these times, before making a decision, it is best to first ask yourself why you undertook this task, venture, course, or whatever it may be in the first place. Sometimes all you need is a reminder to get you going again.

If this doesn't work, search inside your heart to feel if it's right or whether it will help others in some way. If you have started a venture, it is always best to give it all you've got before giving up, no matter what the situation. If it's a relationship, it can be a little more difficult because emotions will be involved, and when they are involved, it isn't always easy to make a rational decision. Sometimes you have to step away and take a little time out, if at all possible, before making a decision. Usually you can feel what's right in your gut or heart.

However, the majority of the time, all you need to do is search inside yourself to find the strength and courage to carry on. Remember the person you are and look at how far you have come. Everyone started somewhere, and most people probably felt like giving up at some stage along the line. What is worse: persevering or thinking 'what if'?

Perseverance shows strength of character and helps to build you up to your highest potential and achieve all you can.

You've got this; keep going!

Finish what you start

Many people have good intentions. They start out full of enthusiasm and energy for something, and then fizzle out before they accomplish what they set out to do.

Sometimes this could be for practical reasons, such as finances, or perhaps there was more involved than they first thought. Other times, it could be that they no longer have the passion like they did in the beginning. This is such a shame because how do you know what you are capable of if you don't see it through to the end?

Seeing something through to the end will not only give you a sense of accomplishment, but your confidence will soar once you realise that you are capable and can achieve what you set out to do.

Whether it's a new course, project, building or renovating a house, starting a business or a venture of some kind, or even a new relationship, give it the respect, time, space, and energy it requires. Everything needs a little room to breathe and a little time to get started. As they say, 'Rome wasn't built in a day.'

It is true that in today's world we are impatient for success. It is easy to think that if it doesn't happen instantly, it means it will never happen. That is nonsense. Have faith in what you do; above all else, have faith in yourself.

Remember you can achieve anything you want to achieve if you put your mind to it. Your mind is not the only thing you need to put into it, although it will give you a huge head start. You will also need energy, sometimes money, a little tenacity, a whole lot of passion, a little determination, and drive.

Go on; see what you can do.

Allow yourself to fly

Many people hold themselves back. They restrict themselves by not allowing their minds to dream big and fulfil their highest potential. Don't do this. Give yourself the gift of soaring as high as you can with whatever resources you have. Do whatever you can to research, learn, and challenge yourself to achieve what you want to do.

Taking risks is part of growing up, growing older, and becoming wiser. If we never took any risks, we wouldn't grow and we would never learn. Think about it. You've been taking risks ever since you were tiny (i.e. when you first learnt to walk), so why stop now? Progress is important. You don't want to stagnate. You want to tell stories about your adventures and the things you have done. Yes, it's okay to boast about yourself now and then, especially when you've earned it. After all, you do deserve it.

Life is not about staying still; there is a time for reaction, and there is a time for action. Knowing which path to choose is just as important as knowing the right time to take action. You owe it to yourself and to others to do and be the best you can be. Success is yours for the taking, so give yourself the best chance in life. Start by putting one foot in front of the other

Follow your dreams

Life is full of possibilities and hope. However, it is up to you to allow these ideas into your life. Only you can decide on which options to take, how fast you want to go, and which way you want to go. It's up to you.

As a child, we listened to our parents or caregivers, and we let them make decisions for us most of the time. Unless you had a rebellious nature, of course, like I did. But most of the time, we trusted them and followed what they said. We let them make the decisions for us.

On the other hand, as an adult, we have to make our own choices in life. It's easy to keep on blaming others, so take the responsibility for yourself and make decisions. This doesn't have to be a daunting prospect. Like most things, it all depends on how you look at it.

So look at it with a sense of adventure and with an element of surprise added in for good measure. Life is a celebration, and the world is here for us to explore in whatever way we choose. Live the life you want to your fullest capacity. Embrace all the good things with love, laughter, and share your joy wherever you go. Don't worry about what might go wrong; instead, think of what could go right.

For you never know what is around the corner and what opportunities lay ahead for you unless you give it your all. Live a life full of possibility, follow your heart, follow your dreams, be kind, and encourage others along the way. Live in the present and make the most of every moment.

Everything is possible; just believe and remember that you can be all you want to be and more if you dare to go for your dreams. It's up to you to make a decision to succeed and take that first step.

Are you ready?

CONCLUSION

Life is a journey of exploration and expression. Embrace the ride. Yes, there will be high points and low ones, but how you deal with these is more important than the points themselves. If you live a life filled with love, joy, peace, harmony, fulfilling work, and relaxation, it will help to keep the momentum going. We all need elements of each of these to maintain a balanced life.

You can choose how you want to live your life; you hold the keys to great success and great love in their purest form. You can be truly happy if you allow happiness into your life. Give yourself permission to live your life to its fullest potential; you deserve the best and all the good things that life has to offer.

As the saying goes, 'the world is your oyster.' You can achieve all that you set out to do and live the life you want. It's all up to you. You are free...

SHARE THE LOVE

Have you found this book helpful?
If so, tell someone about it by leaving a review.
You could help make a difference to someone's life.

ACKNOWLEDGEMENTS

I would like to thank everyone who supported me in writing this book, including my family and friends.

Thank you to Rocky Callen for your encouragement and passion for writing that has helped to keep me motivated.

Thank you to my editor, Sarah Fox, for your continued support, words of wisdom, and guidance on turning my dream into a reality.

You are all amazing and a blessing to have in my life.

THANK YOU!

ABOUT THE AUTHOR

Pamela Sommers is an author and founder of SommerSparkle, an award-winning online boutique that provides beautiful jewellery & accessories for special occasions, which have been showcased in a number of magazines, including *British Vogue.*

Her work has been featured in *Inspired Brides* magazine, *Post Code News* and she has also been featured in the *HuffPost* blog and *House of Coco* magazine, with her tips for entrepreneurs.

Pamela is passionate about inspiring others to make their dreams come true. She loves to listen to music, dance and enjoys horse-riding. She currently lives in London, England with her fiancé and son.

You can find her online at
www.pamelasommers.com
www.facebook.com/PamelaSommersOfficial
www.sommersparkle.com

Printed in Great Britain
by Amazon